Taking Stock

Taking Stock
A Woman's Guide
to Corporate Success

Sharie Crain
with Phillip T. Drotning

Henry Regnery Company · Chicago

Library of Congress Cataloging in Publication Data

Crain, Sharie.
  Taking stock.

   1. Women executives—United States.   2. Women
in business—United States.   3. Success.
I. Drotning, Phillip T., joint author.   II. Title.
HF5500.3.U54C7   1977   658.4'002'4042   76-55667
ISBN 0-8092-8005-1

Published by Henry Regnery Company
180 N. Michigan Avenue, Chicago, Illinois 60601
Manufactured in the United States of America
Library of Congress Catalog Card Number: 76-55667
International Standard Book Number: 0-8092-8005-1

Published simultaneously in Canada by
Beaverbooks
953 Dillingham Road
Pickering, Ontario L1W 127
Canada

To Ewald Nyquist, New York State Education Commissioner, for saying it all:

"When a female Einstein is promoted to assistant professor that isn't equal opportunity. We'll know equality is here when a female schlemiel moves ahead as fast as a male schlemiel."

Contents

Preface

One of my friends commented recently, "I've been in women's consciousness-raising groups for years. I'm *conscious* of all the problems we women face at work. What I need now are *solutions.*"

Her comment really expresses my purpose in writing this book. During more than a decade in the world of work, I have been confronting those barriers. It began even before I finished college, when the corporate interviewers asked my male classmates what kind of training program interested them, and then asked me about my typing speed.

I knew I wasn't qualified to be a typist—hunt and peck won't get you very far in an office these days—but in my own mind I did know I was as qualified for a management training program as my male counterparts. After all, that's what I had been going to college for. But my own opinion of my capabilities didn't make much difference; what I saw when I looked at myself was not what those male interviewers saw. Because I was a woman, all the little bells in their heads rang "typist" or "secretary."

That was my first clue that the rules for this game of business were unlike those of any other game I had ever played. It made no sense that a company would hire me for a job I could barely do—typing—and not even consider me for a management training program I had spent four years preparing for.

Fortunately, I wasn't ready to give up and take just anything the work world had to offer. Since I couldn't find a company that would hire me for a management training program, I did what seemed the next best thing. I negotiated a job. I interviewed with a company that was willing to pay a good salary for a receptionist with a college degree, and I accepted the position only on the condition that the first available management training assignment in the personnel department would be mine. Six months later, with no further training, they promoted me to a personnel interviewer's job.

As it turned out, those six months as a receptionist weren't wasted. Because my job was neither busy nor challenging, I had a fascinating opportunity to study the business game that was being played around me. I began to understand the hidden rules and to observe why some employees were successful in their work while others failed. It was a perception that was essential to my satisfaction and success on the job.

One aspect of this book explores the hidden rules of the business game and how to utilize that system to meet our personal goals and needs. We are then more prepared to achieve success as it is defined in our own terms.

Why is it that most women don't already know the rules? It's because business is a man's game. He invented it, developed it, nurtured it to serve his needs, and has been playing it for a long, long time. So long, in fact, that the game really represents the essence of the whole male culture. This is a natural consequence of male and female roles in human history that might still remain unnoticed if our culture had not developed so that many women now have both the need and the opportunity to get into the game.

Despite this sexist gap, if the rules of the game were obvious and well-defined it would not be difficult for us to learn them. Unfortunately, they're not. They are, for the most part, an unwritten doctrine of male folklore that is largely concealed from women and pervasively intertwined with the whole male cultural system. These rules are so obscure, in fact, that they even escape the understanding of many of the males who participate in the game.

Women, like men, have different reasons for working—challenge, money, the need for self-fulfillment. Perhaps, in some cases, we work because we want authority and power—to become chairman of the board. But whatever the reason, one thing is certain: The very quality of our lives depends upon how we feel about our jobs.

Most books about the role of women in the workplace advocate methods that are intended to change the way the business system works. Certainly the efforts of women's activist groups, governmental agencies, laws, and court decisions have had an impact on business and will continue to do so. As I will suggest in the final chapter, business *will* change over time and women will help change it. But that is of little help to the woman who wants to improve her situation right now. Life goes on, and each day that we spend in an unrewarding work situation, *when we could be doing something to improve it,* is a day of personal satisfaction and economic benefit that has—irretrievably—been lost.

Although the chapters that follow look at the business world from my perspective and experiences as a woman with twelve years in the game, this book is in every sense a collaboration. My almost silent partner is Phil Drotning, a male player whose experience has included responsibility for affirmative action programs in one of the world's largest corporations. He is sensitive enough to cope with the chauvinism that no male in our culture can totally escape, and the book would not be the same without his insight into the effects of that culture on both men and women. I can interpret business only as it has affected me during years of experience as a businesswoman. Phil's contribution adds an essential element—the perspective of a businessman. It makes the picture complete.

Why is his role so important? Because, as the rules are now defined, it is still the men in the corporation who control our ability to get what we want from our jobs. For the most part, it is men who have the power, and we need to learn how to play the game so that we can use the rules to enlist that power to support our objectives. The alternative—spending our working lives frustrated and unhappy, simply because we spent our time in a futile effort to change the rules instead of learning to understand them and turn them to our advantage—is simply not smart.

The attitudes and beliefs of the males we work with are largely beyond our control; in fact, because of our early cultural indoctrination as men and women, they are probably beyond their control as well. But how we choose to deal with these attitudes is largely up to us. This is really a microcosm of life itself. Those who interpret life positively almost inevitably have a more complete and rewarding life experience than those who continually feel threatened and denied, and who perceive every life situation and experience from a defensive, negative position. Epiticus said it in the first century, A.D.: "People are disturbed not by things, but by the views that they hold of them."

The basic attitude that a woman expresses in her work is probably one of the single most important factors in her success or failure. The most superb technical or professional performance—essential as it is—will not overcome the effects a negative attitude can have on how your superiors perceive you. Perhaps even more important, a negative attitude toward your job probably will pervade your other waking hours as well.

That sounds so simple, and of course it isn't. Basic attitudes aren't easy to change, but if it's a positive change it's worth it. This book is filled with tested techniques that will help you find yourself, improve your outlook, and get more from life as well as your job. Many of these techniques have been developed for dealing with very specific work-related problems; others are more general personal growth techniques. For example, as you gain a better understanding of the rules controlling the business game, you may decide that to get a raise or a promotion you must change some of the dynamics of your work situation. Experience has shown that most of our problems as women in business are not task-related. They are emotional issues that involve us and the males around us. This book includes some specific ways to deal with these problems. Once you begin to use them I believe you'll find, as I have, a positive transference to your personal life as well. The conflicts of life will seem more manage-able. Your sense of humor—a most important facet of anyone's existence—will begin to emerge again.

I want to acknowledge my parents' contribution to my own preparation for a career in the business world. They reared an only child and nurtured in me the belief system that anything is possible. They imposed no boundaries on what I believed I could do or be as a female.

They gave me the courage to try, the will to do, the motivation to succeed, and perhaps most of all, a sense of humor that made it all possible.

Sharie Emmerich Crain

Introduction

Whatever your reasons for working may be, you certainly want to make the most of your business opportunities. Perhaps, like many other working women, you don't plan to devote a lifetime to a business career; instead you are working now—or planning to work—because at this stage in your life you need the money. If so, you obviously want to earn as much as possible doing work that you enjoy. On the other hand, if you are career-oriented like growing numbers of other women, your objectives—in addition to money—probably include job satisfaction, appreciation and recognition, status, responsibility, authority and, ultimately, power.

After years of listening to the lamentations of women who turn up faithfully at their jobs each morning and go home discouraged and frustrated each night, I'm convinced that many working women need to know what's in this book. That, in case you haven't kept up with the statistics, is a lot of women—39 million of you, in fact, at the end of 1976! That's nearly two million more than were employed a year earlier, and nearly 20 million more than were working twenty years ago.

In grandma's day, women in business were a rare phenome-

non, and the neighborhood gossips still talked about them—
probably whispering behind their fans. Today, with two of every
five jobs in the United States filled by women, you are an accepted and essential part of the business scene. Census statistics
indicate you also outnumber men, outlive them by an average of
eight years, own more than half of all bonds and nearly half of
the nation's cash and corporate stock, although you may not
always control it. An amazing 90,836 of you are millionaires.

"Interesting," you say, "but I haven't got my million yet, and
the way things are going at work, it doesn't look like I'm ever
going to. My problem is that nobody seems to think women are
very important around there."

And there's the rub. Despite your apparent dominance in
numbers, longevity, and wealth, women as a group haven't yet
achieved the compensation, status, or authority in business that
you deserve. Although Eve has been around almost as long as
Adam, and once generously shared her apple with him, today's
Adams aren't willing to share the fruits of the corporate garden
with her.

You don't need to be told about the problem, because you live
with it every day on a personal level, but you should know the
numbers, if only to have them in mind when you need to prove a
point. They reveal dramatically that if you're dissatisfied because
you seem to be going nowhere, you've got a lot of company in
your rudderless boat.

Today the average pay of women who are employed full-time
is forty-three percent less than the average earnings of men;
$6,800 a year instead of $11,800. Twenty years ago, when only
half as many women worked, it was only thirty-six percent, and
no woman was happy about that. Moreover, the jobs in which
women are predominant are those with the least challenge, the
least status, and the least authority—often simply extensions of
the household chores that women have always been expected to
perform.

If you were a man working under these conditions, it would
make you angry, and sooner or later you'd start raising hell
about it. But you're not; you're a woman and too often women
simply accept job dissatisfaction. But as you will soon discover, if

you don't already know it, the fact that men assert themselves to get ahead in business and women don't is a direct result of the way we have been programmed.

But your future in business need not be grim: The very fact that women are still so far short of their potential in both earnings and responsibility, coupled with the new demands on employers to move toward equal opportunity for women, has opened up unprecedented opportunities for women today.

Current Opportunities for Women

"Today's woman graduate has a better chance of landing a top job and a good salary in business than her male counterpart—no question about it," says J. William Paquette, director of career planning and placement at Drake University in Iowa. His assessment, although not universally true, applies not only to college women whose goal is executive responsibility, but to other women seeking other rewards as well.

If you don't want to sacrifice your lifestyle to the exacting demands of an executive career but still want compensation and appreciation commensurate with what you're willing to put into your work, you can get them if you will use what this book is going to tell you about how to play the business game.

If you are determined to succeed in business and measure success in terms of that long climb upward to the executive suite, the chapters that follow will help you to understand the business system and the men who run it, and they will offer some techniques and strategies Sharie Crain has developed to help you get what you want. I believe you'll discover that it's easier than you imagined, if you are willing to work at it and to make the personal sacrifices that successful male executives have made to reach their goals.

Many business leaders are beginning to realize that they have overlooked an important source of business talent. They are starting to appreciate that during all the years when they have sought "the best man for the job," they should have been looking for "the best person for the job." And that simple change in attitude immediately increases the pool of available talent by well over fifty percent.

Up to now, women have scarcely dented the list of higher-skilled, better-paid jobs. The Bureau of the Census tabulates 250 distinct occupations. Of employed women, half are concentrated in only 21 of these occupations, and a quarter are employed in only five—secretary, household worker, bookkeeper, teacher, and waitress. In the face of the pressures on American business to eliminate de facto discrimination against women, this gives you a lot of room in which to move.

An entire chapter of this book examines the fields that offer the greatest opportunities for you, but let's take a quick look now at those that are wide open to you as you try to get more of what you want from your work.

First, let's look at the professional employment category, where men and women appear to be at a virtual standoff in terms of numbers employed. Men now hold 16 percent of the professional jobs, while 15.5 percent are held by women.

That sounds like a pretty fair shake until you look more closely at the breakdown of professional categories. These totals are deceptive because only 2 percent of men are teachers, while the classroom is the turf of 9 percent of women. The percentage of men engaged in the remaining professional categories, which include the critical business disciplines of accounting, engineering, science, and law, is double that of women—14 percent compared to 6.5 percent. Business is under heavy government pressure to equalize these proportions, and if any of these disciplines interests you, the potential is obvious.

If you are unwilling or unable to invest time and money in additional education, there is a good deal of room for women in the skilled trades—an area they have left virtually undented. At present, twenty-four percent of working men are in the highly paid craft jobs, while only two percent of women are so employed. Here again, under the pressure of federal affirmative action requirements, the picture is changing. Increasingly, women are turning up on the job with toolboxes in their hands. Although the movement of women into the skilled trades is slow, and resisted vigorously by the unions, the opportunity is there if you are tired of typing and filing, want a dramatic increase in pay, and are willing to work with your hands.

At the supervisory and management levels, women are just beginning to make inroads, but again, the opportunity for those of you who want increased responsibility and authority has never been greater. The thrust of federal equal rights enforcement efforts is toward proportionate representation of women at all levels of management and supervision. Note, however, that about fourteen percent of all men now employed are managers, and only four percent of working women. Now for the bombshell: *At present employment levels, correcting this imbalance would open up managerial posts for more than 3 million women.*

New and more stringent laws, regulations, and court decisions have, of course, been a major force in enlarging your opportunities, but other forces are at work too. Business isn't opening doors to women simply because of government ultimatums. How many times, particularly during the recent recession, have you heard disgruntled males suggest that women should quit working so that "male breadwinners" could have their jobs? This rationale overlooks the fact that most working women are "breadwinners" too. Just think what would have happened if all of America's working women had taken that advice. At the peak of unemployment during the recession of 1975, ten percent of the work force was unemployed, and that included both men and women. During the same period, about 37 million of the nation's jobs were filled by women. If they had quit working so that the unemployed—men and women—could go to work, nearly 30 million jobs would have remained unfilled, and business and industry would have come to a screeching halt.

Clearly, employment opportunities for women have increased because, without you, much of the nation's work would not get done. In many instances today women are encouraged or compelled to work because of increased need for additional income, particularly in the case of young couples. There are also greater numbers of female family heads today. Too, the impact of labor-saving household devices and convenience foods has emancipated women from household chores that once required most of their waking hours. Further, the supposed inferiority of women in jobs that require great physical strength is of diminishing relevance in the labor market because technology has gradually eliminated much back-breaking manual work. You might find it impossible to lift a 150-pound carton off the floor of a loading dock, but we'll bet you could quickly learn to operate a self-propelled forklift truck.

More important for you and most other women is the fact that the greatest growth in the job market is in work that offers no inherent advantage to the male. The character of greater proportions of work today is shifting more and more into white collar and service occupations, which you can perform as well as—if not better than—men.

I've dwelt on these facts so that you will read this book motivated by the knowledge that opportunities for you to do almost any kind of work and to advance to the managerial and executive ranks in business and industry are greater than ever before. They may, indeed, surpass those that will exist in the future because corporate affirmative action programs are still in the "catch-up" phase. Whatever one's view of the women's movement, there is no denying that the legislative, administrative, and court actions it has provoked have created a business environment in which many women have a better-than-equal chance to break into new and rewarding fields of endeavor and move upward in them.

Why More Women Aren't Making It

Given such heartening conditions, one would suppose that women would be exploiting their new opportunities to the fullest. The sad truth is that many are not. Fifteen years have elapsed since President John F. Kennedy signed the first executive order prohibiting discrimination in federal employment because of sex, and more than a dozen years since passage of the Civil Rights Act of 1964. The courts have brought some of the nation's largest corporations to their knees, forcing them to pay huge sums in back pay to women employees as compensation for de facto discrimination in promotion practices. In the case of the American Telephone and Telegraph Company, court-imposed settlement fees have approached $100 million.

But despite prohibitions against discrimination, federal investigators and lawyers employed to enforce them, and huge penalties imposed on violators, surprisingly limited progress has been made by women in the work force in the past decade. Why?

Many women I have talked to believe that it is overt discrimination by male executives that is holding you back. I won't argue that such discrimination does not exist, but attacking that constraint will not substantially alter your position in the business environment. Sexism in business, to the extent that it exists, is merely a symptom of a larger problem. The status and roles accorded men and women in the working world are based on *perceived* sex distinctions that grow out of a heritage that considers men "superior" and women "inferior."

We need to do more than simply alter the behavior of the male decision-makers in business and industry. Genuinely equal opportunity for women will come only after we, as a society, have overcome centuries of indoctrination into unequal sex roles, and altered the attitudes, traditions, customs and beliefs of an entire culture.

Obviously the task of radically altering the consciousness of the total society is not one that can be achieved quickly, or even within the life span of one or two generations. But that does not mean that you, as an individual in your own individual work situation, can't harmonize with the *existing* system and work within it to capitalize on the new opportunities that federal pressures on business may have made available to you.

There is no question that women in business are handicapped because you are considered more emotional than men. Most of you have been permitted from early childhood to respond emotionally to difficult situations, to use tears as a safety valve and sometimes as a weapon. Many men, denied this form of emotional release, have concluded that women are fragile, docile, submissive creatures who handle difficult situations with tears rather than action.

What neither sex has fully recognized is that these responses of both men and women are to a large extent learned, rather than innate behavior. Consequently both can be overcome—and must be, if a woman is to succeed in the business environment. Otherwise, the woman who responds emotionally to business situations simply reinforces the man's belief that she is by nature too emotional to deal effectively and rationally with a corporate crisis. She then has two strikes against her in the business game.

And business *is* a game. Like other games it has its own rules, some written, some unwritten. It has its own strategies, some obvious, some subtle, even obscure. It has rigid standards of desired and unacceptable behavior—creeds, taboos, dress codes, rules of speech and appearance. To win at business you must understand the game and learn how to play it. Often, for men as well as women, this requires finding someone who will teach you the game and lead you through it.

Sharie Crain and I have watched women succeed in male-dominated business environments in which most others fail, not because they had superior talent, ability, or training, but simply because they had the initiative and insight to learn the business game. Although one of us viewed the problems of women in business as a man, and the other as a woman, we reached the same conclusions, identifying a number of factors that, if understood by working women, would clear the roadblocks from their path to success. Here they are:

1. Many women are genuinely confused by their new opportunities. They have smarted under the second-class status historically imposed upon them, and they respond instinctively and positively to those who speak for women's liberation. They are also tempted by the promise of more money, status, responsibility, and power. Yet, having observed the sacrifices that aggressive men must make to achieve success in business, many are not certain that managerial or executive status is worth the price they will have to pay to achieve it.

2. Many women are handicapped, to varying degrees, by their own perception of themselves and their appropriate role in society. They find it difficult to escape the mold fashioned by Euripides more than four centuries before Christ: "A woman should be good for everything at home, but abroad good for nothing." As a consequence, they often are inhibited by their male peers and superiors, who are inclined to assume a sort of

divine right to authority and power. Their acquiescence may exclude them from consideration as prospects for advancement.

"There are many companies that are looking for women in top-management positions, but it is the woman's own self-image that must change," says Pam Flaherty, who overcame this hang-up to become vice president of the Citibank of New York. "Fifty percent of the battle is within the women themselves."

3. The progress of many women is also inhibited by their inability to alter the perception of women—or at least of themselves—held by the men in their organization who are in a position to assist or hinder their progress. They inadvertently reinforce the masculine misconception that women are inherently lacking in the psychological and intellectual qualities that are regarded as the foundation of power. They forget that male attitudes, too, antedate Euripides.

4. A great many women in business simply have not yet identified the career paths they wish to follow, the jobs to which they should aspire, and the kind of work they really want to do. The ambitious and determined woman who knows where she wants to go will find allies who will help her get there. But, inevitably, those who don't know where they want to go will go nowhere.

5. Finally, many women have been unwilling or unable to identify and employ the strategies and techniques that have helped their male counterparts up the corporate ladder. In some cases this is a consequence of indifference, or an aversion to increased responsibility, but more often it is because they simply don't know how to find "GO" on the corporate gameboard.

Sharon Kirkman, president of the personnel counseling firm, Boyle-Kirkman Associates, offers one example of how women can learn from male success:

"The first thing an ambitious, young, male executive does is analyze what is rewarded in his company. It varies from organization to organization. It may be certain dress, attitudes, or activities. Once he's identified such things, he proceeds accordingly. Many women—and men—make their biggest mistake by not isolating the behavior that gets rewarded in their organization."

Some working women have no clearly defined career ambitions. They work because they need the money to pursue other activities and goals, or simply to sustain themselves and their families. If this describes your situation, you can still benefit from learning how to maximize your income and enrich your job to make it more fulfilling.

And then there are the 43 million American women sixteen years and older who are not in the labor force, but expect to be sooner or later. Among them are women who have left the labor force for a decade or so to rear their children; others who never intended to pursue business careers but are compelled to do so because of divorce or the death of their husbands, and those still in high school or college who will soon be ready to go to work. If you're one of these, you too can improve the quality of your first job—the satisfaction that it gives you, the opportunities that it offers, and the earnings it provides—if you develop a sound strategy before you even begin to look for work.

What follows will help you to do this. The techniques and strategies are Sharie's and they are presented from her point of view. They are not abstract theory, but practical, tested concepts that have been used successfully by hundreds of women whom she has counselled over the years. They will help you, too, if you apply them conscientiously.

Good Luck!

Phillip T. Drotning

1

Understanding the Male Business System

Most men still believe that their job is to bring home the bacon and that their wives' job is to put it in the pan. The concept is an anachronism, of course, in an era when nearly 40 million of us are doing both—bringing home the bacon and cooking it as well.

Both men and women cling with irrational tenacity to this myth about the distribution of responsibilities because centuries of human history have taught all of us to think that way. And even though recent social, economic, and technological changes have made the concept an absurdity, business remains the ultimate male game. What that means for you and me, unfortunately, is that it has been designed from the beginning to exclude meaningful participation by women.

Every one of us who enters the business game soon observes that its rules, traditions, values and standards capture the essence of maleness in our culture and, in fact, represent the qualities against which male success is measured. The game encourages—even demands—such qualities as assertiveness, competitive drive, cooperative spirit, strategic, logical and analytical skills, and a compulsion to assume leadership and achieve authority and power.

All of these qualities are the ones that are carefully nurtured in males from earliest childhood. The business game has been designed by men to make maximum use of the qualities that are, for the most part, peculiar to males—to bring success to those who have made the most of their "basic training" as males. While motivation, interest, luck or health may have a part in that success, it is how well men have learned the game they were reared to play that leads to success in business. In the process, it also determines most aspects of a man's lifestyle—how well and where he lives, who his friends are, what schools his children attend, even what values his life decisions are based on.

It doesn't happen that way with us. As women we may be motivated, interested, capable and happy to fully commit ourselves to our jobs, yet the game still evades us. Not only has our cultural training failed to prepare us for business roles, it often has not even prepared us to enter into business. The simple truth is that many of us are trying to play a game in which the other team knows the rules and we don't.

Happily, things are changing, and they are changing fast. Contemporary business can no longer survive without us. It is under tremendous pressure not simply to utilize our talents in the traditional capacities, but to open up opportunities for us at all levels in the business community. For the first time in history, we can win in the game if we learn the rules.

We'll only be spinning our wheels if we allow ourselves merely to feel frustrated or guilty or angry because our career progress is clearly less than we deserve. Instead we must learn to understand the game, the culture that produced it, and the attitudes that a lifetime of cultural training has instilled in both men and women. Once we understand these things, we can begin to do something about them.

Those really responsible for reinforcing our own cultural attitudes, of course, are our mothers and, to a lesser degree, our fathers—to say nothing of our mother's mother, and our father's father, all the way back almost to infinity. This is also true of our male associates. From the moment a pink or blue label is attached to us when we arrive in the hospital nursery, girls and boys are programmed by mothers and fathers to assume specific—and very different—roles in society, just as our parents were programmed a generation before.

The process is neither mysterious nor complicated. If you go back to your earliest childhood memories, you'll probably remember being taught that girls should be gentle, submissive, and "ladylike." You will recall that anger was intolerable but tears acceptable; that assertive behavior was discouraged and acquiescence rewarded.

If you showed interest in manual skills (other than those learned in the kitchen) or in team sports, or in scientific and technical knowledge, you probably were discouraged. Mother directed you toward more aesthetic pursuits and domestic skills, the kind of training and discipline calculated to find and please a husband, cook a good meal, keep a neat house, and rear a new generation of children in the same sexist image.

The inevitable result of this indoctrination is that too many of us perceive our role in life as one that is significant only in the negative. If, as women, we fail to win a husband, if we keep a sloppy household or systematically burn the toast or ruin the coffee, we become failures to ourselves and others. We become the woman in the TV commercial who, courtesy of Folger's, is always being rescued by Mrs. Olson. On the other hand, if we succeed in all these things, we are not rewarded—not in the same sense that a man is rewarded for doing well at what the same social order expects of him.

Even in doing the things that are expected of us, we were taught to be passive, to wait for things to happen to us. We were expected to find a good husband, but God forbid that we should be the aggressor. The man must do the proposing, and in the traditional marriage ceremony we would be the ones who promised to love, honor, and *obey*. We were trained from childhood to be dependent, not independent; passive, not competitive.

After marriage, we are ever-supportive of our husbands, and our identity becomes dependent on them. We gain stature not from what we do but from what our husbands do. For the most part, our reward in life is his approval, which may be no more than occasional acknowledgment that our daily drudgery is appreciated. "That was a good dinner, dear," he says absentmindedly as he plops himself in front of the television set or settles down with the newspaper or with work he has brought home from the office while we go back to doing the dishes.

No wonder it's hard for a woman in this culture to develop a truly independent identity, a true sense of worth! From puberty on, we seek achievement by finding an achievement-oriented man. Our identity is established through him. The major strategy our environment teaches us is the manipulative strategy required to catch a man and keep him, and even this strategic skill is rarely appreciated because it fails if the man is aware of it.

True, because of consciousness-raising efforts growing out of the women's movement, these attitudes have been modified in recent years, especially among young people. But most of the authority in today's world still rests with people who were taught to think, and still think, this old-fashioned way. The extent to which it affects each of us may vary. But it's very difficult for even the strongest-willed woman to escape it entirely.

Now consider what was happening to our brothers while we were being cast in our humble mold.

The ideal male qualities, in the eyes of society, are physical strength, manual dexterity, physical coordination, independence, competitive instincts, personal courage, and aggressive leadership talents. These are symbolized by the father who visits his newborn son in the hospital nursery carrying a baseball glove.

Even as a little boy the male who cries is told to stop and "behave like a little man." Anger and aggression in a male child are seen as harbingers of "manliness." Small boys are encouraged to engage in physical activities and are exposed in the Little League to organized team sports. Fathers buy them boxing gloves so they can learn the "manly" art of self-defense. They are permitted to climb trees and indulge in other risky adventures that would be unthinkable for their sisters. They learn early to play together as a group and to sublimate individual achievement to group effort. In these situations, they also learn to lose, as well as to win, and to accept losing in the knowledge that they'll have another chance to win tomorrow. They are encouraged to learn the manual and technical skills on which society places a premium, and to pursue studies that will increase their value in the nation's job market.

The impact of these differences in the childhood conditioning of boys and girls is pervasive throughout our lives. Every quality a boy is encouraged to develop and every skill he is required to learn are among the qualities and skills that are required for success in business and industry. Meanwhile, those instilled in girls—passivity, dependence on others, aversion to risk, and emotional responses to difficult situations—are certain to make a woman's progress in the business environment extremely difficult.

The result of this sex-oriented socialization process, which is fortified in later years by the teachers, counselors, clergy, and virtually everyone else we meet, is that most men enter the labor market prepared for the competition of the business world and women don't. On arrival, the man can count on the advice, counsel, and support of males already in the business world who will guide him through the system and teach him to be effective.

Women who go to work find themselves in a man's world, and most of us are psychologically and emotionally unprepared to compete with men because this is precisely what we have been taught *not* to do. When we were born, we weren't all that different from men, psychologically or emotionally, but society did a remarkably effective job of making most of us different. As a result, women who enter the business world today are attempting to play a game that is the essence of maleness; a game that we women have been skillfully prepared by our culture *not* to play.

You have probably been taught to behave, react, and think of yourself as the traditional family-oriented, uncompetitive woman, and to regard men as the aggressive, career-oriented achievers. On the job, this affects the way you think about yourself and the way you think about men. Men, who have been trained to perceive you and themselves as opposites, are in a similar situation.

The important thing we have to consider is not how this affects your career development, but how you can work around it. Remember, you were *taught* to be what you are and men were *taught* to be what they are.

Unless a woman who enters business understands that she is really trying to learn poker in a game with a stacked deck, the odds are overwhelmingly against her. To succeed, you must improve the odds; you must learn to understand the system, the men you work with, and most of all, yourself. That is what this book will help you to do.

Begin by Analyzing Your Own Personality

The last few pages have presented a sort of composite of the cultural influences on the attitudes and behavior of men and women. Obviously, they don't all apply to everyone, so before you can plan the strategies that will enable you to get what you want from your work, you will find it helpful to discover precisely what impact these cultural influences have had on you and how your current behavior patterns are affecting your work life. Understanding the attitudes and behavior of the men who dominate your work environment is as important as understanding yourself.

The Success Profile (Table 1) will help you to do this. The profile was drawn from analysis of the personality characteristics of women who have already succeeded. By comparing your responses with those of already successful women, you can quickly identify some behavioral traits that may be causing you some difficulty—and you aren't even aware of them. Complete the profile as honestly as you can, but don't spend a lot of time on each question. Your instinctive response will probably be more accurate than one you have paused to consider.

This success profile (don't read on until you have completed it) is based on research by Dr. Bruce Ogilvie at San Jose State University, who has conducted many studies of successful men and women. To prepare it, he surveyed 300 women in various fields —everything from art and sports to business and politics. Each woman was given 1,300 questions to answer, and from the replies Dr. Ogilvie summarized the personality traits most consistently displayed by women who had made it to the top of the organizational ladder.

The responses in the right-hand column are those that fit the "success" profile. Those on the left don't. All successful women, of course, don't exhibit all of the traits cited in the right-hand column, but they are more apt to have most of them than not. And, of course, some of them are more important than others.

Table 1
Success Profile

I tend towards being an	☐ introvert	☐ extrovert
I show my anger	☐ with difficulty	☐ easily
I enjoy sticking with problems till they are solved	☐ true	☐ false
I am basically easy going	☐ false	☐ true
I will do almost anything to get attention	☐ false	☐ true
I enjoy	☐ following	☐ leading
I want to make a good number of friends	☐ true	☐ false
When threatened, I	☐ retreat	☐ attack
Guilt often bothers me	☐ true	☐ false
Social approval is important to me	☐ true	☐ false
I generally wait for things to happen to me	☐ true	☐ false
I tend to be	☐ cautious	☐ impulsive
Close attachments to people are	☐ important	☐ unimportant
To control my emotions is basically	☐ difficult	☐ easy
I enjoy new fads and fashions	☐ false	☐ true
Confrontation is	☐ difficult	☐ easy
I get bored quickly	☐ false	☐ true
I enjoy doing little things for people	☐ true	☐ false
I enjoy physical and emotional risk	☐ false	☐ true
I will make a great contribution during my life	☐ false	☐ true
Competition is	☐ distasteful	☐ enjoyable

The profile shows, first of all, that the successful woman tends to be an extrovert. People don't frighten her and she's completely prepared to fight when she knows she's right. She has no fear of confrontation when she considers it necessary to achieve her objectives. This, remember, is not typical female behavior. Since childhood, while boys resolved critical disputes with a punch in the nose, girls were taught to pick up their dolls and go home. Yet that's not winning behavior in the world of work.

Along with her willingness to engage in confrontation, the successful woman expresses anger without feeling guilt or remorse. And when angered, or threatened, she is apt to attack. This, too, is the antithesis of the traditional woman's reaction. The stereotype is that women are used to seeking protection. When threatened, many women may retreat. That won't work in the business environment if you choose to get ahead, because your ideas and proposals and actions are constantly being challenged. If you fail to defend them, you aren't doing what you are paid to do.

In other situations, too, the successful woman rarely feels guilt. She is basically independent, and she is usually sure she is right. She can fire an inadequate subordinate without feeling guilty and wondering whether she was somehow responsible for his or her failure. This degree of confidence in one's own judgment is critical in business because people with a strong sense of guilt are apt to avoid making difficult or unpleasant decisions, however crucial they may be. In business, not making a decision is usually a bad decision from the employer's point of view.

Like successful men, the successful woman usually does not enjoy following through on specific problems or projects from start to finish. She enjoys the creative process of finding a solution, but when implementing that solution becomes dull and routine she's ready to move on to something else. She won't leave the job undone but probably will skillfully arrange to turn the final execution over to others.

Most women who make it up to the top are relaxed and easygoing. This is consistent with the demeanor of male executives who make it to the top, while the intense, nervous, worrying personalities get stuck somewhere in middle management. The worriers are usually the people who finally pick up the dull pieces that successful executives leave behind.

At some time during her career, the successful woman has

acquired the leadership drive common to successful men, and she strives to gain authority because she really dislikes taking instructions from others. Typically, she is not a joiner because she does not enjoy being part of a group she can't lead, or one which has rigidly defined rules or guidelines.

The successful woman generally has many acquaintances but few close friends. She avoids close attachments that may interfere with her freedom of action or put constraints on her behavior. She is not concerned about social approval, except the approval of those who can aid or impede her future personal growth and progress. This trait sets her apart from most women, who are reared to believe that it is important for them to please others and be liked by them.

This stereotype woman has a difficult problem that is rooted in her upbringing: her self-esteem becomes dependent on pleasing others, usually men, and she fails to develop an independent self-identity. Her identity is so unformed that she tends to reflect the desires of the person she is with at the moment, particularly if that person is a man. She is Bill's wife, or John's daughter, rather than herself. Men, on the other hand, begin to shed this need for social approval during late childhood and the adolescent years, when they are gradually permitted to escape the rigid parental guidelines of childhood and to develop initiative and self-reliance, which are regarded as desirable traits in a male. Thus, they begin to see themselves as having worthwhile identities of their own.

Successful women don't wait for things to happen to them; they make them happen. Too often others do little to shape their own destiny, but are manipulated by circumstances. You can prove that to yourself by recalling the major events in your life and determining how many of them you consciously planned and how many resulted from the actions or influence of others, or from unforseen events. Women don't decide to get married; we wait to be asked. We don't demand a raise; we wait for the boss to give it to us.

Because we have been programmed to wait, we are not inclined to take the initiative in work situations. Successful people try to anticipate the demands of their job and the needs of their employer. The losers in business are the ones who wait timidly to be told what to do.

The successful woman tends to make quick decisions, often

intuitive and not well thought-out. Of course she makes occasional mistakes, but she gambles that her successes will outweigh her failures. She has learned that even a bad decision is often better than no decision at all. Many of us, fearing error, will search for the perfect solution until, in desperation, our boss makes the decision for us.

Typically, the successful woman gets bored easily. Whenever anything becomes routine, she wants out. She enjoys new, exciting experiences; she thinks new fads and fashions are fun.

Perhaps because so many of her peers are cast in supportive business roles, the successful woman does not enjoy doing what she considers unimportant things for others. As a secretary, if that is where her career begins, she typically resents getting coffee for her boss or doing the Christmas shopping for his wife. She will find ways to avoid these duties until she has attained a position where they are no longer expected of her.

She is able to refuse to perform demeaning chores because she has the courage to take risks—something many women are too cautious to do. In large measure, this is because she is exceptionally self-confident and views risk-taking positively because she does not concede the possibility of failure. Less self-assured women view risk-taking negatively, and are deterred by the possibility of failure, rather than stimulated by the potential for success.

Finally, the successful woman enjoys competition. And competition, of course, is the essence of business success. She is confident that she has important contributions to make in any endeavor that interests her, and will challenge anyone—male or female—in her desire to prove it. This is atypical behavior because most women are not comfortable in competition *with* men, but only in competition with other women *for* men.

How Do You Stack Up?

Now that you have studied the characteristic traits of successful women, you are in a position to compare them with your own.

If you analyze the results of your own profile objectively, you may find significant differences between your personality and behavioral characteristics and those of the successful women on whom the profile was based. You might also note that these characteristics are remarkably similar to those you would expect to find if a successful man had taken the test.

In a report on the 100 top corporate women in the United States, published in *Business Week* on June 12, 1976, the editors made the same observations:

"These 100 women who wield corporate power are distinguishable for only one thing: They are indistinguishable from their male counterparts in how they came to their present business eminence."

If you choose to try for the top, let this be the first discovery on your path to success: Everything in your male competitors' experience has been calculated to prepare them to succeed in business. Your ability to compete with them, as has been the case with other determined women, will depend to a large degree on your ability to understand how the game of business works and play it well.

This does not mean that you should surrender your feminine qualities that could make the conduct of business more sensitive and perceptive. Nor does it mean that you must abandon your own value system, which may include ideals that are sometimes lacking in business, ideals that could help the corporate world overcome its present negative image. What it does mean is that right now, while you are trying to be successful in a man's world, you need to develop and use the same tools that enable men to get there.

What Your Success Profile Will Tell You

Spend a few minutes comparing your choices in the success profile with those made by successful women in the column on the right. You will recognize many of their choices as obvious characteristics of success, but others may surprise you, so let's analyze them closely to see what it takes to be a business success. You will have discovered that she seems consciously to have eliminated from her behavior most of the traits that men commonly ascribe to women, and to have assumed those that are typical of and highly regarded by men. She avoids behavior that will reinforce the male concept that she is emotional, lacking in career motivation, accepting of a subservient, supportive role, timid, passive, and preoccupied with insignificant details. She cultivates behavior that will establish her as assertive, courageous about taking risks and engaging in confrontation, ready to attack if threatened, and eager to take on new and difficult challenges.

It is revealing to note that a large percentage of successful women enjoy a significant advantage; they are "only daughters," or the eldest of all-daughter families. It is easier for them to develop assertive, self-assured characteristics because they often were not as rigidly stereotyped as most girls when they were children.

These women, unencumbered by a brother whose opposite they were expected to be, often developed what our culture considers both male and female personality traits or behavior patterns. Generally, because their fathers had no son on whom to lavish attention, they shared with him many of the experiences—fishing and camping trips, athletic activities—that would have been denied them if a boy had been around.

A woman reared in these circumstances has an obvious advantage in the business environment; she is better prepared initially to play the game because she has already learned many aspects of male behavior. If this is your situation, you're lucky.

You can start rehearsing for a successful business pattern right now by not letting *this* challenge scare you!

2

How to Win in a Male Environment

Now that you have looked at your personal success profile, it's time for a more searching look at your male competitors so that you can learn to deal with them successfully in the male-dominated business world.

I hope by now that you recognize that business has always been a man's game, with women playing a supportive role. This division of responsibility goes all the way back to primitive humans, whose survival needs depended on the use of the male's greater physical strength to hunt, fish, fight and ultimately plant, harvest, and build. It was a distribution of labor that was supremely rational in a more primitive era, but one that has become an anachronism in an intellectual and technological age.

Unfortunately, we are still living with these consequences of history, whether they make sense or not. The woman who wants to enjoy her work must learn to understand and play the male business game. We have no choice, because, as we have seen, the traits that are considered ideal in the successful business person are obviously male since the business game is fashioned in the image of the male segment of our culture.

Consider the male hero image in our culture. It reflects most of the traits of the successful business executive, traits, in fact, that most of them have. The male hero image is that of a cool, independent, and self-assured man, utterly without emotional vulnerability. He is a leader, totally goal-oriented, undistracted by personal considerations that would interfere with the job at hand. His concentration on results is so intense that he is rarely distracted by feelings or human concerns—sympathy, compassion, guilt, jealousy, or revenge—that might divert him from his ultimate objective.

To understand fully how the typical businessman got this way, let's look again at the socialization process. In our early and most formative years most of us depend primarily on our mothers. They fulfill our needs for food, warmth, cleanliness, comfort, and love. At this stage, because their fathers have yet to become deeply involved in their lives, boys as well as girls form strong attachments to their mothers. This continues until they begin to walk and talk and develop a distinct personality, at which point the boy is discovered by his father.

Now suddenly, without warning, he is taught that he must not be like Mommy, the very person with whom he has identified throughout his first two or three years. Not only is he instructed not to be like Mommy, he may actually be punished if he displays feminine qualities that he has observed in her.

The experience is traumatic, and to cope with it a typical boy learns at a very early age to repress many of his emotions. He is told repeatedly that little boys don't cry, just little girls cry. He is also taught that little boys are strong, aggressive, and outward. He is encouraged to venture into the world and learn to explore and manipulate it. Later he is introduced to competitive team sports, where he learns not only the importance of winning but also of losing gracefully. If, before his teens, he becomes preoccupied with reading, or collecting stamps, or other intellectual rather than physical pursuits, his parents may worry because he is not developing as a typical boy.

During these formative years boys spurn girls; they may be unconsciously conditioned to regard us as inferior. Girls, meanwhile, although we may be allowed to play with boys, are encouraged to retain the sensitivity and the emotional characteristics imparted to us by our mothers. These are the tomboys among us. They may wrestle with their brothers, but unlike the boys they may also cry if they get hurt. Eventually, as children move into adolescence, the boy's aggressive, explorative, competitive behavior is encouraged, while the tomboys among the girls are usually directed toward more feminine pursuits. Their former male playmates view them with increasing disdain, and, however competitive they are, when sides are chosen they are no longer picked for the team.

This is usually the period when boys learn to become goal- and achievement-oriented. They aspire to become heroes— which often, in their adolescent eyes, means being a star on the high school football team. A high school football star is the idol of the girls and a hero to other boys, and he epitomizes most of the competitive characteristics that are rewarded for growing up male in our culture.

At this stage of development, most of us, even the tomboys, begin to shed our masculine traits and are taught to make our- selves attractive to men. Our competitors are no longer the boys we once wrestled with, but other girls. The quintessence of achievement is to capture the attention of the football star. He is attracted to the girl because she is the essence of femininity; she is attracted to him because he is the epitome of the male ideal in our culture. The girl who captures this prize is probably very attractive, supportive, and superior in all the qualities that soci- ety expects of a woman.

These remain the ideal male and female roles as we move into adulthood. The boy, as he becomes a man, is enjoined to control his youthful impulsiveness, to settle down, to become mature. He is taught to be more rational, analytical, objective, detached, and impersonal with other males. He is still encouraged to set goals and compete vigorously to achieve them, because this is essential training for the next competitive arena—the world of work.

During this period, the woman typically becomes a settling influence, further establishing her male-supportive role in soci- ety. Surveys have shown that when men are asked why they got married, the typical response is that they were leading a wild life and knew they had to settle down sometime. They thought a wife would be a stabilizing influence. Very few mention love as a reason for marriage. In one survey of over six hundred men, only eleven percent said that they loved their wives. (I wonder how many wives of the men in this group could say that they loved their husbands!)

The adolescent girl, as she matures, is under increasing pressure to become dependent, supportive of men, and passive and fragile so that she will be attractive to a man whose ego-need is to be her protector. If she completes high school and goes on to college, the odds are heavy—even today—that she will be steered away from the academic disciplines most valuable in business, and toward those seen as supportive of her future role as a wife. On graduation, our culture has everything planned so that male and female needs mesh, at exactly the same time, because the traditional sex roles have been clearly defined. The man will enter the business world, for which his ideal qualities have equipped him well, and the woman will stay at home and play the traditional role for which she has been reared. Historically, she has been accepting of the cultural precept that it is the man who is dominant, authoritarian, rational, aggressive, decisive and protective. She has been taught to be none of these, so the husband and wife who fulfill society's ideal complement each other very well.

Although the male has been the dominant figure traditionally, the supportive role of the woman was extremely important and even necessary in the past. Upon marriage, the male gradually drifts out of his long-time male friendships. His life is now primarily devoted to the pursuit of business and the needs of his wife and family. Not only has his wife kept his house and reared the children, but she has become his principal emotional support as well.

Actually, this dependence of men on women is so acute that it can be measured statistically, as an aspect of physical health. Recent data indicate that the death rate of divorced males is three times that of divorced females. Another study showed that, among widowers, the death rate from coronary artery disease was forty percent above the norm during the first six months after the death of their wives. Other studies have shown that bachelors have a suicide rate more than four times that of spinsters; that divorced males are more inclined to rush into new marriages than divorced females.

While men continue to be terribly dependent on women, the women in their lives are becoming increasingly less dependent on them. Many of us are entering business and succeeding in it by recapturing the innate traits that we had before we were socialized at puberty. We are denying the fantasy that we are fragile, helpless, and dependent, and we are rejecting our role as the supportive member of the marital team. We are striving successfully for an independent identity and for recognition for achievements of our own. The divorce rate has soared toward fifty percent as increasing numbers of wives resist the authoritarian dominance of their husbands and discover that they can do without them very well.

Although most of them are not consciously aware of it and few would admit it if they were, men feel frightened and threatened by this evolution of the independent female. They need their marriages and see them as threatened by the emergence of women from their traditional role. They are preoccupied with their own prospects for success in business, and they sense that with more women in the competition, their career objectives are threatened as well. The independent woman in business epitomizes all of men's fears rolled into one person. She becomes a threatening symbol of unwelcome change.

To make matters worse, because of his social orientation, the man is totally unprepared to deal with this new breed of liberated women. How can he compete with a woman who challenges his traditional authority while he is still handcuffed by a social orientation that says he must protect her? He has been taught that his is the dominant sex, but now finds himself competing with, and perhaps supervised by, a woman.

Until now, most men have accepted women in business because, with rare exceptions, we have been in supportive roles. Now, they find themselves uncomfortable with those of us who have broken out of the clerical or secretarial ranks. The established ground rules of business conduct are inadequate when women are introduced into the equation as independent beings.

An example is the business lunch or golf game, during which men discuss business, sports, politics, and other personal topics, always carefully preserving their masculine image. Add a woman to the discussion and the men are uncomfortable because they are now in a situation not covered by the old set of rules. Some of them will be spurred by the sexually competitive instinct that is aroused when an attractive woman is involved. Others will try to preserve the old game by ignoring their female associate and pretending she isn't there. Still others will direct the conversation in ways intended to push the woman back into her traditional, stereotyped role. They may pointedly compliment her dress or perfume, or the way she has done her hair— all remarks intended to remind her that she is a woman.

Men are also uncomfortable with ambitious business women because we bring feelings into the business equation. From a very early age, as we have seen, boys are taught to submerge their feelings, to deal dispassionately and unemotionally with problems and events. In the business environment most successful men continue to repress and even deny the whole range of human emotions in order to act the acceptable masculine role.

As a consequence, he takes a pragmatic approach to every business situation and usually rejects all other possible routes because they are, to him, unpredictable and intangible. They make him feel threatened and vulnerable because he is not prepared to deal with them. He is therefore troubled by the ambiguity of not knowing how to act or respond to a woman on a peer level, because he doesn't know the rules of her game. He is confused because he is accustomed to thinking in binary terms: Things are either black or white, good or bad, profitable or unprofitable, and, until now, male or female.

Dr. Tobias Brocher, of the Menninger Foundation in Topeka, Kansas, conducts seminars for corporate executives on problems of stress. He says many of the men he talks to admit that they feel threatened by women managers, in part because women already have one. capacity that men don't. They can bear children. When women demonstrate that they can also do "men's work" as well as or better than men can, the prospect is frightening for their male associates, and particularly for their husbands.

"More often than not they give in to their unhappiness," Dr. Brocher reports. "The fact that their wives don't need to work makes it all the harder. They feel uncertain about their role as providers—a loss of power is implied. And, above all, they have a sense that they don't really know their wives after all. It's very unsettling for them."

To succeed in business at any level women must have the support of men who are already there. To get it, we must understand the dynamics of male–female interactions in business and their effect on the game. We'll spend some more time on this subject in later chapters.

3

Fields of Maximum Opportunity for Women

Many of us are hampered in our business careers because we have been led to pursue a single-minded objective: We are taught that the ultimate goal is to be married. As a consequence, many of us do not plan our lives with careers in mind. Who needs a career plan when your prince will come and you will marry and live happily ever after?

This cultural game plan has worked well for a great many of us who are comfortable in a supportive role and do get married, do raise fine families, and do live happily (some of us in the shadow of our husbands) forever after. And of course those of us who live this kind of life are indispensable to our social order as it is now constituted. But marriage has severe shortcomings as the sole objective of a woman's existence in a world in which increasing numbers of us elect not to marry, even more elect not to have children, and nearly half the marriages end in divorce. Our culture has no real answer for those of us who are one day shocked to discover that 1) there is no prince, 2) the prince is poor and stays that way, 3) he is an intolerable partner, 4) he dies, or 5) he runs off with his secretary (a supportive type who also learned her manipulative strategy well!).

Too many of us, confronted with one of these departures from the game plan our mothers laid out for us, find ourselves unprepared to build an independent and rewarding life outside of marriage. No one had ever suggested that we develop an alternate plan except, perhaps, that we learn to type as an "ace in the hole."

Dr. Margaret Hennig helped to set up the first graduate program for women in management at Simmons College in Boston in 1974. In some early research she and a colleague studied 108 women executives and concluded that, while women may work all of their lives, few of us begin to regard ourselves as career women before we reach the age of thirty. Because we have not been taught to plan a future other than marriage, we are often more concerned with security than progress, and so we remain locked into dead-end jobs. Typically, we are likely to concentrate totally on the job at hand, without giving a thought to what lies ahead, or even to what we might do to improve our current situation. Besides this, because we have been taught that business is a man's game, many of us expect to fail. Predictably, we do—because our attitude and behavior make failure inevitable.

This general lack of career orientation in childhood, other than planning for marriage, is responsible for a major problem we have. Many of us find our opportunities limited because we lack the specific training, education, and skills that are essential in many of the more lucrative business careers. This is true even among those of the 108 women executives who indicated, in their youth, a high aptitude for some of the more sophisticated business-oriented disciplines and skills.

For example, Dr. Lois Graham, a professor of mechanical engineering at the Illinois Institute of Technology in Chicago, has observed that "a girl who is good at mathematics is still likely to end up being directed into teaching." How many secondary school teachers, counselors, and parents steer women into engineering?

But studies show that two-thirds as many females as males among eleventh grade students tested have engineering aptitude. It's obvious that lack of professional and technical training among us is due less to any deficit in potential ability than to education, counseling, and socialization processes that direct us away from such careers.

The consequences of inadequate business career counseling are evident in our educational choices. One study of college majors selected by women found nearly two-thirds enrolled in majors that have little relevance in the business community. Nearly 21 percent were in the humanities, 6.5 percent in the social sciences, 4.2 percent in fine arts, 29.5 percent in education, and 5.5 percent in home economics. Only a third were enrolled in engineering and the physical sciences, business, medicine, and other nonteaching professional and technical fields. For males the situation was almost exactly reversed, with more than two-thirds enrolled in business-related specialties, and less than one-third in nonbusiness fields.

This distinction is critical because, while education and training in specific skills determine the level of work you can do, and consequently your salary and future opportunities, college diplomas do not have equal value in the business world. A B. A. in art history, for example, is virtually worthless in the business world, unless you work for an art dealer; its only value is as evidence that you had the initiative to complete four years of college. On the other hand, a degree in engineering demonstrates that you have knowledge and skills that can be put to use immediately in many business enterprises—and, particularly since you are a woman in today's environment, you will be highly sought after.

If you want to work in business and industry, you should think very carefully about the kind of education and training you want. Many of us are tempted to settle for training in typing and secretarial skills, perhaps because it takes less time and costs less money, and because there is always a great demand for secretarial and clerical work.

If you are not interested in a long-term career, if you plan to work because you need to make some money for a while, or if you want a job that won't intrude on your lifestyle, being a secretary may be a good choice for you. But before you make this choice, be aware of its limitations.

Getting ahead in most business organizations is the result of on-the-job training in a succession of increasingly responsible jobs, each of which adds not only to your experience and knowledge but to your range of skills. While secretarial work allows you to improve your initial skills, it doesn't add many new ones. So, your progress will be measured largely by the money you make, and perhaps by the status of the man you work for. Eventually, even if you are the best secretary around, you will peak out at the salary level your company regards as the maximum for secretarial work.

Many young women, for example, make this choice, even though they know its limitations, because their ultimate goal is marriage, not a career. When, for some reason, they don't get married, they find themselves locked into the job. They have the option, of course, of selecting a new career path and making the sacrifices necessary to get the education and training they need to pursue it. But by this time, going back to school or getting more training seems difficult, and most of them elect to settle into a secretarial career for the rest of their working lives. If that's what you want, fine. Just be sure you aren't cutting yourself off from something better.

Lots of women never enjoy business or advance in it because they lack any commitment to the business world. Usually this group is marking time until they can stay home, since they get little satisfaction from their working life. Few of us realize that, even if we marry, we probably will spend much of our lives working at some kind of job. The average for working women is about twenty-five years. If you're smart, you'll prepare yourself well, because you may very well have to go to work because you have no other choice. Of the 39 million women now working, nineteen percent are widowed, separated, or divorced, twenty-two percent are single, and twenty-five percent have husbands with annual incomes below $7,000. Obviously most of us aren't just working because we want to, but because we must.

The lack of commitment on the part of some of us unfortunately can affect the opportunities of all of us, because it reinforces the belief of most men that we are not really interested in our jobs. The woman who prepares herself specifically for business in a field such as engineering, for example, is more apt to be dedicated to a business career and more likely to continue in the work force without interruption. She also will be perceived by men as having greater commitment to her job.

Ideally, every woman, even if she does not intend to pursue a lifetime business career, would prepare herself as though she did. You always have the option of quitting work and settling into the routine of a permanent, even happy marriage. But if you haven't prepared yourself, and something happens to your marriage, you probably don't have the option of stepping into a personally and financially rewarding business career.

This emphasis on education and training doesn't imply that you can't find rewarding opportunities without them, but simply that it's easier if you have them. There are many areas of opportunity in today's job market where women without specific educational skills can not only get a job, but advance and prosper in it.

Commission Sales

One such job category is commission sales. In this kind of job you get a minimal base salary that is supplemented by commissions on the merchandise you sell.

Commission sales work has a number of virtues. The first is that, except in the case of highly technical products and services, generally you need no specific education or experience to get a sales job and succeed in it. Your success or failure depends on your motivation and your personality traits. If you are outgoing, if you enjoy people and talk to them easily, if you have confidence and determination, and if you're a real self-starter, you have the basic components to succeed in sales.

The second virtue of commission sales work, for an ambitious, energetic, and personable woman, is the fact that where earnings are concerned, the sky's the limit. In sales, unlike most entry level corporate jobs, you aren't locked into a rigidly structured salary schedule. Your earning potential is based on your productivity and, if you're good at sales, it could exceed what you would expect to earn after years on the typical corporate job.

Both Phillip Drotning and I have several acquaintances without business degrees, not long out of high school or college, who are earning $40,000 a year and more in commission sales. David King, president of Careers for Women, operates a sales training course for women in New York City. The first group of women who took his short-term training course averaged about $30,000 a year during their first year of sales work.

Commission sales is also an ideal field for many of us because it offers immediate feedback on how well we're doing. Many women have difficulty in adjusting to the business environment in the early stages of our careers. We have no basis on which to judge how effective we are, other than the feedback we get from those around us—and those we work for, who are usually men. If we're unfortunate enough to work for men who have negative feelings about women in business, the feedback is apt to be negative. We may begin to feel that others are expecting us to fail, and then we become the victim of self-fulfilling prophecy.

This simply means that if our peers or our bosses indicate, even subtly, that they don't think we're performing well, we'll feel under greater pressure to perform and may begin to make mistakes. The mistakes then confirm their belief that we are not performing well, and the downward spiral continues.

In reality, our performance may have been fine, but we had no way of knowing it. In commission sales you can measure success or failure on a real time basis, day by day. You know precisely what sales volume the company expects of an effective sales person. If your sales equal expectations or exceed them, you know at once that you're doing a good job; you're not dependent on others to evaluate your performance. The knowledge that you're doing well, in turn, raises your level of confidence, and this, in turn, helps you to do even better. This is the positive side of self-fulfilling prophecy, which is now working to your advantage to give you immediate positive feedback on how effective a job you are doing.

The best jobs for women are often those with *quantifiable accountabilities*. That may sound like a mouthful, but it simply means having measurable goals on which to judge your performance. In fields such as personnel or public relations, you deal in intangibles, and performance measured on a subjective evaluation of your efforts. This sometimes works to a woman's disadvantage, because performance evaluations are usually made by men, and, as we've already seen, their judgment may be negatively influenced by their expectations of women.

The more measurable the results of your work are, the more certain you are of getting credit for them—and of being noticed when you are really good. Your progress is less dependent on the subjective judgment of others, because the quality of your work can be measured in quantifiable terms. And with quantifiable objectives, you have the opportunity to establish credibility early in the game. Once your reputation as an effective performer has been established, your peers and supervisors are more likely to view you in that light in the future. Once you have established a good reputation, it's relatively easy to maintain it, but if you are perceived from the outset as ineffective—which is often the case with women whose first boss is hung up on the female stereotype—you'll have an uphill battle to change that image.

Commission sales has another advantage: It is easier than many other occupations for a woman to break into. Many employers still regard us as dilettantes where work is concerned. They hate to invest money in training us, because they're afraid we'll soon get married and quit our jobs because we have babies or our husbands are transferred. In commission sales work, relatively little training and development time is involved, so the loss to the employer is nominal if the women they hire decide to leave early in their careers.

In addition to immediate financial rewards, sales careers also offer women the opportunity to climb a well-defined career ladder. Most sales organizations are organized in groups of increasingly larger units, each with a management structure at the top. The organization will vary from company to company, but typically it will have local sales teams, which report to district sales offices, which report to regional sales organizations, which are responsible to the corporate headquarters sales group. At each of these levels, there are supervisory and management slots, with increasing responsibility and authority vested in those who occupy them as you move up the organizational chart. The woman who wants to improve herself in this organization not only has a broad range of opportunities, but she can also pinpoint precisely the next step in her upward progression, and prepare herself to attain it if she so desires.

Although more and more of us have been breaking into sales work in recent years, we are still relatively few in number—excluding the Avon lady, of course. The fact that saleswomen are still a novelty in many product and service lines is a definite advantage. Often we're able to make appointments just because the buyer has never had a woman call on him before. He may simply be curious, but that curiosity offers the saleswoman an opportunity to get her foot in the door. That's often more than half the battle where sales work is concerned.

This advantage works best if you choose a nontraditional product to sell. The more unlikely the product, the greater the impact of a sales approach by a woman.

Women are apt to succeed in sales because it requires creativity, ingenuity, imagination, and even intuition, and all of these traits are stereotypically possessed by women. The object of sales work obviously is to convince someone to buy something, and we're often terrific at devising new and ingenious ways to do this.

One woman in sales was having difficulty getting an appointment with a potential customer who was inundated with requests from competing companies. She tried every conceivable approach, including repeated invitations to lunch or coffee, without success. Finally, she decided to try something totally new. She called the customer and, after commenting that he had consistently refused to see her because he was too busy, suggested that she bring a picnic brunch to his office.

The customer was so startled that he apparently decided he had to see it to believe it. The saleswoman appeared at his office with a picnic basket, spread a table cloth on his conference table, and served rolls and coffee while she made her sales pitch. By the time he had downed the last roll and finished his coffee, she had a new account.

Her success, once she got in the door, may have been partly due to another advantage that women sales reps appear to have. Many potential customers have become hardened to what they regard as the "slick salesman" image, which conveys a lack of credibility. This doesn't extend to the female sales rep, not only because she is unusual, but because in this case some elements of the female stereotype work to her advantage. Men typically are less wary of women because they think of us as more naive, honest, and trustworthy than males. So customers are likely to be more open, less defensive, and easier to convince.

Sales work is so attractive to many women for several reasons: It can give you the chance to work with people, it contains some glamorous elements—a company car, perhaps, an expense account, and often travel—and it offers maximum independence, short of being self-employed.

For women who value independence, sales can be perfect. Unlike normal office situations, sales activity usually is virtually unsupervised, except for reports and occasional sales meetings. Depending on the job, it may offer opportunities for traveling all over the country, and even abroad. Many sales people work out of their homes or apartments, appearing at the office only for sales meetings. They can determine, in most cases, the hours they want to work, because the employee's efforts are not measured by time but by results. Obviously, however, this freedom and flexibility means that you'll need a great deal of self-discipline.

Beyond the opportunities that sales offers for moving up in the sales organization, you have a chance for lateral movement into the marketing field. You may have to go back to school for some marketing courses, or even a degree, but it will be well worth it if you're willing to invest the time and effort.

The umbrella term "marketing" describes a number of functions that complement the company's sales effort. The major ones are advertising, promotion, and market research. Not only is sales an excellent background for this type of work, but in many companies sales experience is required of anyone who moves into this type of job. Marketing should appeal to you if you're a particularly creative woman.

Sales may be an especially good choice if you're an older woman who has reared her family and is returning to work. Typically there are no age restrictions, and maturity can be a distinct advantage. It offers maximum employment security because it's almost recession-proof. When business is bad, few companies lay off their salespeople; it is those employed in less essential staff support functions who find themselves out on the street. Beyond that, the skills acquired in sales can be applied to almost every other aspect of your life, most of which is spent selling something, even ideas.

Production Supervision

It may surprise you, but another fertile field for women is that of plant or production supervision. During World War II this was a common occupation for women, but in more recent decades women rarely have held these jobs, except in a few selected industries. That has changed.

As with sales, many corporations don't have specific educational requirement qualifications for production supervision. Even if you majored in Byzantine history in college or home economics in high school, you probably can qualify for a job in plant supervision. Even so, it's a promising entry-point for women who are pointing toward management jobs. Most companies offer training for these positions, which largely involve the supervision and motivation of unskilled employees who work at assembly line jobs.

Because production management is not a traditional assignment for women, it allows the really determined woman to quickly become a star. Your superior performance can be soon noticed, because in your job you're surrounded by members of the opposite sex. That is obviously not the case in occupations traditionally inundated with females.

Production supervision offers a great variety of jobs and almost unlimited opportunities for employment. Next time you enter a department, drug, or hardware store, notice the incredible array of products on the shelves and counters. Recognize that behind each of those products is a group of industrial workers, and each of those groups reports upward through a structured supervisory and management organization. Because there are so many supervisory and management jobs in the field, and so few women presently performing them, the competition at the entry level and even beyond is far less intense than in many other occupations.

Once you become a production supervisor, you've already circumvented the whole clerical function, which for most career-oriented women is a dead-end street, and you've opened up a whole range of promotional opportunities. Clerks, typists, and secretaries rarely move out of this supportive activity into broader fields. In production supervision, you may accomplish in weeks what it would take you years to achieve in another occupation, if ever.

If you like working with people and want, ultimately, to get into personnel work, for example, production management can be a good place to start. It offers more opportunity than most other occupations to work directly with people. You counsel the employees in your department; you motivate them, help them solve problems that may be interfering with their work; you hire them and fire them if the union will let you. In the process you may develop a whole range of new interpersonal skills or improve on those you have.

Actually, it's excellent preparation for a career at any level of management. At this entry level, you begin immediately to deal with the kinds of problems that top executives deal with daily on a larger basis. It's because of this that production management is looked upon by executive management as such an important step in the career ladder. Once you've learned to manage people, motivate them, and get along with them at this level, you've gained skills that apply as you advance in the organization to any level. It's not the number of people you supervise that is important, but the skill with which you supervise them. Once you've developed this skill, it will be a critical factor in your progress for the remainder of your business career.

Production supervision should appeal to many women because, if you think about it, it is rarely dull or routine, as is the case with many of the traditional business roles of women.

Because you are supervising people with different problems and different personalities, each day offers new challenges. One day you may have an employee discipline problem to handle, and the next day you may be training a new worker. It's an action-oriented responsibility.

Opportunities to move upward from your first job as a production supervisor are excellent. You'll probably begin by supervising a small department of only a few workers. After you have demonstrated your ability, you can move to a larger department, then on to supervision of several sections. This ladder could take you to the top position in the plant, and from there to the top position in one of the company's larger plants, or perhaps to the corporate office.

Your experience could also take you to a position in personnel, or in one of many other staff functions. As you sharpen your skills in one area of management, you'll have a chance to gain skills in others. You now have become part of general management with the opportunity, depending on your abilities or limitations, to move all the way up to Chairman of the Board.

(You see what a useful book this is. You've hardly begun reading it, and you're already at the top!)

As a rule of thumb, you will usually find that the pay is better in occupations that traditionally have been filled by men. Consequently, your compensation in production supervision will probably be significantly greater than in a field traditionally reserved to women—secretarial work, for example. Although companies may place a premium on jobs traditionally performed by men, the Equal Pay Act requires them to pay you what they are paying men for performing that work. This is important in terms of present income and of what you can earn as you move up the management ladder.

If you are interested in moving up that ladder, there is another less apparent advantage to beginning your career in a production plant. First, the fact that you are "not afraid to get your hands dirty" immediately rids your male associates and supervisors of many of the stereotyped notions they have about women. More important, a great many men in the upper levels of corporate management also started out as plant supervisors. They will respect you more because they are aware of the skills you have developed to become a successful supervisor.

Your job as plant supervisor also provides maximum exposure, not just to those working for you, but to other supervisors and the middle and top management of the plant. You are in less danger of being hidden in the ranks than those women who make traditional career choices.

Would You Enjoy Production Supervision?

If you like a lively, active, and sometimes noisy physical environment, enjoy work that produces visible results, prefer an informal atmosphere, and are outgoing and like people but can also be firm and decisive with them when necessary, production supervision may be for you.

I have asked many women plant supervisors what trait they considered most important for a woman in this kind of work. Almost without exception, they said she needs a good sense of humor. Many of the women noted that the better your rapport with the men you supervise, and the more they respect you, the more jokes they play on you. It seems to be their way of telling a woman boss that she has been admitted to the club and that they think she's a "good guy." One recalled being told by one of the men that she had a telephone call. When she picked up the receiver, there was no one on the line, but when she hung up there was a big blob of grease in her hair. Even though she was a mess, she laughed it off, because she knew that the gag was really a vote of confidence.

A woman who chooses production supervision because it is a routine management ladder and expects to get ahead should also realize that she has made a career commitment. Advancement in any company requires dedication to your work. Managers don't get very far if they watch the clock. Those who succeed work overtime when it is necessary to complete their work, and many of them take their jobs home with them. This is not intended to discourage you, but rather to help you decide whether this type of work and possible commitment is for you.

What Kind of People Do Companies Look For?

Evidence of career commitment is of primary importance to employers, particularly where women are concerned. They want plant supervisors who project an image of good judgment, have a background of responsible performance, and appear to have self-confidence and the ability to get along with others. A real plus is experience that indicates leadership qualities which, in the case of a woman who's never held a job before, could be indicated by political activity, for example, or service as an officer of a social or professional organization.

If you're seeking a position as plant supervisor in a company that has never before employed a woman for this capacity, it's important to let interviewers know that you are aware of what the job entails, and that you are sincerely committed to succeeding at this kind of work. They may raise questions about your capacity to adjust to a male environment—how you might react to lewd jokes or profane language, for example. Make sure they know you are aware of this kind of thing and that you can handle it.

Skilled Trades and Crafts

Historically, jobs in the skilled trades and crafts, which are heavily unionized, have been reserved almost exclusively for men. As noted earlier, only two percent of women workers are now in craft jobs, compared with twenty-four percent of the men. Yet there is no question that many of us have the aptitudes and potential skills for this kind of work. We proved it during World War II, when about seven million women entered the labor force, and when almost three million of us broke into such occupational categories as craftsmen, foremen, and other skilled manual positions. We proved that we could compete effectively as shipfitters, machine operators, welders, and in a host of craft jobs.

In that era, women were sought for that kind of work because military needs had drained away the normal male labor supply. When the men returned from the war, the women, for the most part, returned to their kitchens. Today, under the pressures of equal employment regulations, employers are again seeking women for the skilled trades. This is a good choice for you if you enjoy manual work, much of which may be performed out-of-doors, and if you have the aptitude for it. Projections for employment in the 1970s indicate that apprenticeships in the skilled trades will increase rapidly. So, this is an excellent escape hatch for women who are in dead-end, low-paid traditional jobs.

What Is an Apprenticeship Program?

1. An apprenticeship program is usually learned through a combination of training and work on the job.
2. It is clearly identified as a specific skill that is recognized throughout industry.

3. It involves manual, mechanical, or technical skills and knowledge that require a minimum of 2,000 hours of work and training, including the time spent in work-related instruction.

4. It requires related instruction to supplement the on-the-job training. This instruction may be given in the classroom, through correspondence courses or self-study, or by any other means of instruction that is approved by an administrator.

5. It involves skills broad enough to apply in similar occupations throughout industry, not those restricted to the products of any one company. These skills may include those of cooks, cosmetologists, florists, bakers, watchmakers, draftsmen, carpenters, plumbers, and electricians.

What Do You Do As an Apprentice?

When a company hires you into an apprenticeship program, you agree to undergo training on a schedule provided by the firm. This training schedule will include on-the-job experience in the various skills that are related to the trade you are pursuing. This training program will be carried out under the close supervision of skilled craftsmen. The remainder of your time will be spent in instruction that uses the latest techniques and equipment to supplement what you learn on the job. In most cases, this is carried out under an agreement with an educational institution.

Apprenticeship training continues for about four thousand to eight thousand hours, depending on the skill being learned and your aptitude for it. This involves a period of two to four years, which includes 144 hours a year of classroom instruction. During this time, you will be paid as though you had a regular, full-time position with the company.

The Advantages of Apprenticeship for Women

If your career opportunities are limited by your lack of training in any specific skill, and you can't afford to go back to school to get it, you may want to enter an apprenticeship program. As I have noted, employment opportunities are growing in this area. Between 1972 and 1985 it is estimated there will be an increase of 2.2 million jobs in the skilled trades.

Through apprenticeship, you can learn a skill at the company's expense, and be paid for your time while you are doing it.

What's more, the skill you learn is one that does not restrict you to one company; it's required in almost every type of industry. This gives you lots of flexibility in choosing where and for whom you will work.

Once you have a skill that industry needs, your future employment problems are solved, barring a national economic catastrophe. If you wish, you can move across the country and find a job there. If you are dissatisfied with one employer, you can apply to another. If you get bored with one industry, you can quit and choose another. Because they are heavily unionized, the skilled trades generally offer the highest wages in industrial employment below the management level. Once you have completed an apprenticeship program and become a journeyman, your earnings will be in the range of $20,000 a year—and substantially higher if your job workday includes overtime.

How to Get Into an Apprentice Program

Most companies give apprentice tests to those who apply for these programs. These tests are heavily math-oriented and may be quite technical. If you are not strong in these areas, you might write to the Bureau of Apprenticeship and Training, Department of Labor, in Washington, D. C., to find out whether there are any pre-apprenticeship training programs in your area.

Self-Employment

If you cherish your independence, if you believe that you have entrepreneurial skills and instincts, and if you're not afraid to take a risk, you may want to go into business for yourself. Consider this seriously only if you have already had experience in management, and have gained substantial competence in the business you want to enter. The odds against a new business venture are enormous under the best of circumstances—about seventy-two percent fail within the first two years—so you'll want to evaluate your prospects very carefully.

Studies have shown that women (and men, as well) who choose to go into business for themselves do so because they have a strong need to achieve, a fierce drive for independence, a desire for job satisfaction, and the economic necessity to do so They believe that, as an owner, they can escape taking orders from others, will develop an acceptable self-identity, and enjoy the achievement of developing a business from scratch. Often they are successful managers who have become disillusioned by the limitations placed on their creativity by mature industrial organizations.

The problems associated with succeeding in a new business venture are enormous, and there's no room to deal with them here. If this avenue attracts you, I can only urge that you study the abundance of literature that is available, and that you consult with as many female entrepreneurs as possible before you commit your capital, credit, time, and energy to a business of your own. You might, for example, seek information and advice from the Small Business Administration, from groups such as SCORE (Service Corps of Retired Executives), and from nonprofit economic development corporations such as Advocates for Women in San Francisco.

Greatest Opportunities by Type of Industry
Current projections indicate that the following categories of employment will offer the greatest opportunities for women in the future: finance; consumer products; merchandising and retailing; real estate, building, and construction; entertainment; and the public sector.

Best Geographical Areas for Women
Currently, the East Coast and California have a preponderance of the most highly placed women in industry. The most promising cities for would-be women executives are New York City, Washington, D. C., Atlanta, and Los Angeles—and, as you might surmise, advancement opportunities for women seem to be greater in large cities than in small ones.

Best Opportunities by Size of Corporation
Large corporations and corporations doing substantial business with the government appear generally to offer the greatest op-

portunities for women because of federal pressures for equal employment opportunity. There's evidence, however, that while you may find it easier to get a nontraditional job with a large corporation, you may advance more rapidly, and to higher levels, in a smaller one, where your performance is more likely to be noticed and rewarded.

In this chapter I have enumerated for you: fields in which upward progress can be made without specific education or skills training, occupations in which substantial growth is expected in the next decade, and, fields in which women are not yet well represented. These fields offer you the greatest prospect that your achievements will be noticed, and in these fields you can climb the corporate ladder and earn maximum compensation, while facing minimal competition.

I have not attempted to cover jobs available in the traditional areas of female employment, on the assumption that you know about these already or that lots of information about them is already available. My major contention is that the woman who really wants to achieve in business—whether her objective is job satisfaction, greater income, more responsibility, or authority and power—has a better chance if she enters a nontraditional field.

Business in the past, as we have seen, has tended to provide supportive roles for women and more responsible and better-paid positions for men. If you want to get ahead in business do not go where all the women are. Point yourself toward the traditionally male business preserves, because that is where you'll find the greatest prizes.

4

How to Choose a Career That Suits You

Many of us devote a lifetime to work we don't enjoy and for which we are inadequately rewarded, because we don't direct our own lives. If this happens to us, we don't have a firm self-image because we have been culturally indoctrinated to think of ourselves in relation to others who are usually male. We are someone's wife or someone's girlfriend or someone's mother. Too often, we become so involved in these roles that we never get around to analyzing ourselves in terms of who we are, what we really enjoy, what our goals are, and who we want to be.

Because of our early training, most of us have never learned sound decision-making skills. Trained from childhood to be passive, we let others make our decisions for us and let circumstances determine where our lives will take us. How many women do you know who took a job because it happened to be available, spent years complaining about it, but did absolutely nothing to improve their situation?

Successful women, for the most part, are those who—although they were not equipped to do so in childhood—have learned to set goals and priorities and then plan to attain them. If you have had a tendency to let circumstances and other people determine the direction of your life, maybe it's time for you to recognize this. The best way to do that is to decide which goals are important to you, take a realistic look at what you really want to do with your work life, and set orderly priorities for getting where you want to go.

Those of us who are victims of the Cinderella syndrome, without knowing it, spend our lives waiting to be rescued. Let's assume that you sometimes feel that way. In this chapter, I'm going to try to prepare you for the possibility that you won't be rescued because the prince's stallion broke his leg and he isn't coming to your aid. Doing this is going to take some cooperation from you because I'm going to provide an exercise that will help you identify your real career preferences and goals so that you can begin immediately to plan your life on your own.

Specifically, complete the self-analysis survey in Table 2, which will give you information you need to determine your aspirations in relation to your work and your total life needs and objectives. With that information in hand, you can then analyze what you want from a career and determine which one would be most rewarding for you. Having determined this, you are ready to develop a personal action plan that will provide an orderly process for finding the position you want.

Turn now to the self-analysis survey (Table 2) and complete it, following the directions. Remember, the purpose of this survey is to increase your own awareness of yourself; there are no right or wrong answers. Don't be surprised if some sections of the survey force you to spend some time thinking about what really is important to you. That's part of the process, so take all the time you need.

You may be surprised at some of your answers. Most of us have never stopped to consider, in an orderly way, our hopes and desires, likes and dislikes, needs and aspirations. Some elements of the survey go to the very core of your personality, and it may take some soul searching to complete them. When you are comfortable with the way you have answered the questions, go on to the analysis section that follows. Please don't read the analysis before you complete the survey because it may distort the survey results and lower its value to you.

Table 2

SELF-ANALYSIS SURVEY

Life Priorities

A. List those parts of your life that are important to you. Some examples may be family, leisure time, status, spiritual growth, learning, personal relationships, work satisfaction.

\#   \#

— _____   — _____

— _____   — _____

— _____   — _____

— _____   — _____

— _____   — _____

— _____   — _____

In the space on the left, number them in order of importance to you.

B. Now review them again and think five years into the future. List those parts of your life that you think will be important at that time.

\#   \#

— _____   — _____

— _____   — _____

— _____   — _____

— _____   — _____

— _____   — _____

— _____   — _____

Now number those in the order you think they will be important to you.

Life Roles

A.   List all the different roles you have in your life at this time. (For example, wife, system analyst, mother, cook, etc.)

#	Role	#	Role
—	_____	—	_____
—	_____	—	_____
—	_____	—	_____
—	_____	—	_____
—	_____	—	_____
—	_____	—	_____

Think about the importance of each role to you. Number them in order of importance to your life.

B.   Look at the roles you have listed and think about each of them five years into the future. Some roles may be temporary and may not exist in five years; other roles may be new. List the roles you think you will have in five years.

#	Role	#	Role
—	_____	—	_____
—	_____	—	_____
—	_____	—	_____
—	_____	—	_____
—	_____	—	_____
—	_____	—	_____

Think about the importance of each role and number them in the order you think will be important to you in five years.

Work Needs

A. List those work needs that are important to your job satisfaction.
    For example, financial security, self-esteem, achievement, social
    and business growth, and learning.

#	Needs	#	Needs
—	_____	—	_____
—	_____	—	_____
—	_____	—	_____
—	_____	—	_____
—	_____	—	_____
—	_____	—	_____

Number these needs in order of importance to you.

B. List the work needs that you think you will have in five years.

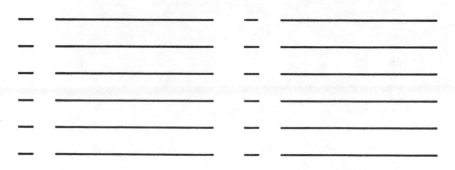

Number them in order of the importance you think they will hold
for you in five years.

Work Preferences

Check your preference:

1. I prefer to work with:
   ☐ people
   ☐ information
   ☐ a product

2. I enjoy working:
   ☐ alone to produce a result
   ☐ on a team effort

3. I prefer to:
   ☐ sit at a desk
   ☐ be mobile in my work

4. I am a:
   ☐ leader
   ☐ follower

5. I enjoy:
   ☐ detailed work
   ☐ the "big picture"

6. I would rather have:
   ☐ a fixed salary
   ☐ an incentive system of pay

7. Business competition is:
   ☐ enjoyable to me
   ☐ unpleasant for the most part

8. I would prefer to work with:
   - ☐ mostly men
   - ☐ mostly women
   - ☐ unimportant

9. I prefer:
   - ☐ routine assignments
   - ☐ variety in my work

10. I enjoy:
    - ☐ taking a risk on a business decision
    - ☐ a virtually "no-risk" job

11. I think I would prefer:
    - ☐ a large company
    - ☐ a small company

12. I prefer a business environment to be:
    - ☐ formal
    - ☐ informal

13. I want to work:
    - ☐ 8 hours a day
    - ☐ more than 8 hours a day if necessary

14. I want a:
    - ☐ job
    - ☐ career

15. I think I would enjoy:
    - ☐ a nontraditional position
    - ☐ a traditional female occupation

16. A pleasant working environment is:
    ☐ important to me
    ☐ unimportant to me

17. I enjoy:
    ☐ learning new skills
    ☐ perfecting existing skills

18. I enjoy:
    ☐ persuading people
    ☐ being persuaded

19. I prefer:
    ☐ security in a job
    ☐ a risky, high-potential position

20. I am looking for:
    ☐ more responsibility in a position
    ☐ minimal responsibility

Now number in order of importance the ten work preferences that are most important to you.

Job Activities Analysis

Analyze all positions you have ever had. List your major job activities, estimate the percentage of time spent in each activity, and then rate your degree of interest in each activity.

Job Analyses

Title

Job Activities	Percentage of time	Very High	High	Some	Low	None
			Interest			

Title

Job Activities	Percentage of time	Very High	High	Some	Low	None
			Interest			

Title

Job Activities	Percentage of time	Very High	High	Some	Low	None
			Interest			

Title

Job Activities	Percentage of time	Very High	High	Some	Low	None
			Interest			

Title

Job Activities	Percentage of time	Very High	High	Some	Low	None
			Interest			

Work Skills

(as you believe your supervisor would rate them)

	Excellent	Good	Fair	Poor
Verbal Ability				
Writing Ability				
Typing Ability				
Math Ability				
Steno Ability				
Planning Ability				
Decision-Making Ability				
Analytical Ability				
Efficiency				
Organization				
Attention to Detail				
Follow-Through				
Work Independence				
Motivation				
Effectiveness				
Dependability				
Initiative				
Assertiveness				
Creativity				
Enthusiasm				
Conscientiousness				
Adaptability				
Loyalty				
Handling Pressure				
Attitude				
Cooperation				
Leadership				
Helpfulness to Others				
Diplomacy				
Others				

How to Analyze Your Survey Results

If you did a thoughtful job of completing the survey, you probably began to see some patterns even before you finished. Review the results in depth and see what they tell you about the importance of work in your life and the type of work that will be most satisfying to you.

Life Priorities

Analyze the aspects of your life that you listed as being important to you as life priorities. How many of them relate to your working life? How high did job satisfaction rate in your priorities? Do the results indicate that you consider work a more important part of your life than most other activities? If so, your priorities appear to be such that you will profit in terms of life satisfaction by investing in education or training that will enable you to pursue a career that involves important responsibilities and a possibly heavy commitment of time and effort. Management could be your ultimate goal. On the other hand, if the results indicate that job satisfaction has a low priority for you, this kind of investment of money, time, and effort may not make much sense for you.

Don't overlook the possibility, however, that your present interests may change as your situation changes over time. That's why you were asked to list the things that you thought would be important to you five years hence. Look at them now. Are they the same as the initial responses or has job satisfaction assumed a greater importance? If it has, you still may want to consider preparing for a more involved career.

Life Roles

Look at the various roles you perform now. Pay particular attention to the importance you attached to your work role now and five years in the future. Does the importance you gave it square with your previous notions about the type of job you want? This also may tell you how much you should give to your work in terms of commitment, time, and energy.

Work Needs

Career satisfaction depends heavily on identifying your work needs and giving priority to them. If you're not happy with what you're doing, it may be because your work needs are not being met. That may mean that you should be moving on to something else that fits your priorities better.

The ability to determine work-need priorities is important in choosing among alternate career opportunities. If you know what your work needs are and the priority you attach to each of them, you can then evaluate potential jobs to see which offers the greatest promise of career satisfaction. For example, if your primary work need is job security, you probably shouldn't go to work for a fledgling company that is constantly having trouble meeting the payroll or one with seasonal personnel needs; or, if your ultimate goal is power, it might be unwise to begin your career as a file clerk.

Look carefully, also, at your projection of work needs five years from now. This will help you to select a job now that will lead to job satisfaction in the future. For example, if income is your primary need, rather than status or responsibility, you should obviously point toward work in which the primary reward is a financial one.

Work Preferences

Your work preferences indicate more specifically what type of position you would be most satisfied with. Determining whether you prefer working with people, information, or products will tell you a great deal about the position that will give you the greatest satisfaction. If you like working with people, you might look at jobs in personnel, sales, public relations, or supervision. If information is your bag, you will want to consider research, systems work, accounting, bookkeeping, or editorial work. If you prefer something more tangible, like working with visible products, you might consider work in the skilled trades, product engineering, or manufacturing.

If you concluded that you like working alone and also that you want to be in a nontraditional field, the skilled trades again may be an answer because then you are responsible for your own output, rather than that of a team. You might also consider a nontraditional field like truck driving, where you can have all the solitude you want unless you can't resist your CB radio. Conversely, if you indicated a preference for working in a team, you might consider working for a large corporation where almost everything represents a team effort. If this appeals to you, it may be an advantage you should utilize, simply because the cultural development of most women does not lead them to consider working in a team.

Obviously, if you enjoy working at a desk, almost any kind of office work will fill this need and, having decided that, you can look at your other preferences to decide what kind of office work it should be. If you prefer more mobile employment, you can look at fields such as plant supervision, sales, and even the skilled trades, where you are constantly in motion. Some people like pushing pencils and some people don't.

If you like to lead people, almost any type of supervision or management job is an obvious choice, and your problem will be to select an entry-level job in a field that interests you, which will lead to management opportunity. If you are happy only when you are working under close direction, you might as well forget about management jobs.

Other preferences you should explore before you decide that management and upward mobility are your objectives include your willingness to compete with others for promotional opportunities and your desire for work that could involve responsibility, risk, judgment, self-confidence, persuasiveness, leadership, creativity, and perhaps a total career commitment.

Look very carefully at how you feel about risk, because the willingness to take risks with minimal fear of the consequences of failure is a major attribute of successful managers. If you are unduly cautious by nature, as many of us are reared to be, you might be initially uncomfortable in a management job. In fact, risk-taking is an ability you probably would need to develop to have any degree of management success.

Another consideration, in defining your career objectives, is whether you want to work for a large organization or a small one. Large corporations offer broader opportunities in a greater variety of specialties and, typically, provide higher compensation, particularly in the form of employee benefits. However, it's more difficult to be noticed in a large organization (unless you're the only woman there), work is more specialized so that individual jobs offer less variety, and the atmosphere tends generally to be more structured, formal, and sometimes stuffy. Look again at your work preferences to see which type of organization suits you best.

The amount of time you are willing to spend at your job is critical in terms of your future advancement. If you are interested in moving up the business ladder, it's very possible that you will work more than the prescribed eight-hour day. You may often find it necessary to take work home at night. If you have other life priorities that preclude such commitment, this point deserves serious consideration. You may even begin to resent the intrusion of work into other aspects of your life and end up unhappy with both. There are trade-offs involved here, not a black and white choice, and you'll have to decide which of your preferences you are willing to sacrifice in order to get others that are more vital to you.

A careful analysis of the ten business preferences that are most important to you will provide insights into the type of employment you should consider. Don't expect the result to be clear-cut, because there will be conflicts. Much of life is a matter of trade-offs, and you must resolve them by attaching priorities to each of your preferences and making the choices that give you the most of what you want.

It is probable that, as the result of your analysis, your preferences will put you into one of two major categories. You may discover that your primary interest is your job and that job satisfaction will require that you move upward, assuming risks and responsibilities, learning new functions, and perhaps competing with others to attain success. The other major alternative choice may be work that is more routine, involves no commitment beyond the normal workday, offers security, and meets your financial requirements.

Job Activities Analysis

Study carefully your analysis of the content of previous jobs and the one you now hold. Pay particular attention to the degree of interest that each job activity held for you. You may discover, as many women do, that you have spent years in jobs that held little or no interest for you. If so, you may want to consider turning your career in a new direction.

Work Skills Analysis

Your ability to make a new career choice will depend to a large degree on your present skills and those you are willing to spend time, effort, and perhaps money to acquire. The work skills analysis will help you objectively determine your own strengths and weaknesses. In this section, you are also asked to rate your skills the way you perceive that your supervisor would rate them. Do you agree with that rating? If not, ask yourself why you and your supervisor have differing opinions about your performance. Is the supervisor unaware of your efforts and effectiveness? Aren't you communicating well? Have you perhaps been deceiving yourself?

If you have given a "fair" or "poor" evaluation in any category and you agree with your supervisor, try to identify the reason for your mediocre performance. Is it because you lack experience, training, or direction? Is the skill one which is inherently difficult for you or is this one aspect of your work you just don't give a damn about?

Matching Your Career Interests with Specific Jobs

If you have completed your self-analysis carefully and evaluated it conscientiously, you should now have a fairly complete picture of what your work needs are, what aspects of your work you find satisfying, what work preferences you have, what your life priorities are and where career satisfaction fits into your total life picture, and what your work skills are.

With this added understanding of yourself, your next task is to match this knowledge with information about occupational opportunities, to determine what your specific career path should be. The right kind of job in a field that meets your needs and interests is the secret of a satisfying work life. If you are unhappy in a job, the odds are that you won't be successful in it either.

Your task now is to learn everything you can about opportunities in the world of work. You will probably find that you can
learn a great deal simply by talking to others about the work they
are doing. You may also get help from an employment counselor, but I'd recommend that you try a more structured approach and spend a day in your local public library.

The library will almost certainly have on its shelves two books
that provide a gold mine of career information. One is the *Dictio-
nary of Occupational Titles*, which is actually in three volumes. The
third edition, published in 1965, is the latest. This reference
book, which many consider to be the bible of vocational fields,
lists over thirty-five hundred job titles and covers approximately
twenty-three hundred occupations. Don't let that put you off
because you won't have to read all of them. The three volumes
are organized so that you can identify careers by interest area,
educational requirements, aptitudes, working conditions, physical demands, etc. There is also a volume called *Training and
Method of Entry,* which describes how to break into any career
field that interests you.

The other book is the *Occupational Outlook Handbook,* which
covers 850 occupations in clusters of related jobs. Thirteen basic
clusters are covered: industrial products, office services, education, sales, construction, transportation, scientific and technological, mechanics, health, social sciences, social service, art design,
and communication.

Specific jobs within each of these groups are described, with
details on the nature of the work and the duties involved, so that
you can determine the activities you would be engaged in on a
day-to-day basis. In a section on "places of employment," the
handbook also describes the industries in which you are most
likely to find a particular type of job and the geographical areas
in which the job is most likely to be found.

A training section covers qualifications for employment and
advancement, the educational background required, the entry
point, and the career path leading to a given position. This section can be a real help because it enables you to determine which
jobs you are now qualified for, what qualifications you will have
to develop to seek others, and the personal characteristics you

should have to be effective in each job. You can match these with what you've learned from your self-analysis survey and pick the jobs that are right for you.

Finally, the handbook will provide information on the future job outlook for each kind of work, the level of earnings you can anticipate, and the working conditions you can expect.

After your day of library research, you will have compiled a list of prospective jobs that fall into two categories: Those for which you are already qualified and those that interest you but which would require additional preparation. If you need a job at once, you will have to opt for one of the former type, but you do have the option of picking a job in the same field, a better job to which you can aspire after you have gotten some additional education or training.

If your research leaves you confused or undecided about the career path that is best for you, it will help to do a decision analysis. In a vertical column, list those variables you have identified as being important to you in a job—your work priorities. Then, attach a numerical value to each one, on a scale of one to ten. For example, if income is your primary concern, it might be assigned a value of ten. If you are not very concerned with security, for example, it might have a value of only one.

Next, in a horizontal column across the top of the page, list the jobs that seem to appeal to you most as the result of your research. When you have done this, go through them one by one and consider how nearly each job meets each of your work needs. Again, attach a numerical value to the answer on a scale of one to ten. Multiply that number by the number assigned to each of your work needs. Enter the total in the appropriate square on your chart where the career choice column and the work needs line meet.

When you have done this, you will have a vertical column of numbers under each of your career choices. Add each column and you will quickly recognize which of the career choices will most adequately meet your total work needs at this time. The example indicates the process for two of the four job possibilities. It is clear that sales, with a score of 301 points, is the better choice for the needs listed. This is a very effective technique for making a decision among alternate choices ranked against another special set of factors. You'll probably find many opportunities to use it as a guide in making difficult decisions.

Once you've settled on one or more jobs that excite you, you'll need to identify specific companies to which you can apply, and to determine the geographical area where you want to work. All of the normal employment resources can help you here, but you can also do some further research of your own in Dun and Bradstreet's directory and Poor's *Register of Corporations*.

Putting It All Together into a Personal Action Plan

Now the major part of your self-analysis is complete, you've established your career interests and where they can be fulfilled, you're ready to develop a personal action plan. Actually, you've already completed half of it by identifying your needs, desires, and priorities. The next step is to establish specific, measurable, and achievable personal goals and a time frame for meeting them.

Use Table 3, at the end of this chapter, to complete your personal action plan. The first step is to identify a specific career action that you will achieve in the next six months. State precisely what you intend to accomplish, e.g., "I will do what is necessary to be promoted to supervisor in the next six months," not "I want to receive a promotion." However, your goal should also be achievable or you won't take it seriously. Don't set the goal of being Chairman of the Board in six months unless you expect an inheritance that will purchase a controlling interest in your company's stock.

Your goal should also be a challenge to you, one that will require you to take actions to help you grow and improve your skills. Goals are stimulating when you commit yourself to activities that will motivate you to make your very best efforts. Your goal should also have a realistic time limit within which you promise to achieve it. If not, it will probably remain forever a dim hope for the future. It should also be action-oriented.

It's important, in stating your goals, that you use active-tense verbs and complete thoughts. Don't describe things you won't do. Make positive assertions instead.

Once you have established your goal, it is essential to develop a strategy for achieving it. Begin by listing the obstacles that may hamper you in reaching your goal and how you will act to overcome these obstacles. Then list the specific steps you will take to reach your goal. Now identify people who can help you reach it and describe the help they can provide. Finally, list some friends or co-workers with whom you can share your objectives and ask them to help monitor your progress.

When you have completed devising your personal action plan and begin to implement it, you'll need to develop a method for measuring your progress. Research has shown that only one in twelve who fail to chart their progress regularly reaches the goal that was established. Depending on what your objective is, you may be able to do this by recording the percentage of your goal that is achieved each week or by making a subjective evaluation of progress on a weekly basis.

If you haven't already finished it, complete your personal action plan before you go on to the next chapter.

Table 3

Personal Action Plan

Career Action Project:

I.　State as exactly as possible a specific career action project that you will achieve within the next six months.

_____

_____

_____

_____

_____

Developing a Strategy:

II.   List those obstacles that will hinder your efforts to reach the above goal. List actions you will take to overcome each obstacle.

Obstacles   Action/Solution

_____   _____

_____   _____

_____   _____

_____   _____

_____   _____

_____   _____

III. List those specific steps you will take in reaching your goal.

_____

_____

_____

_____

_____

_____

IV. List others who can be helpful in achieving your goal.

Persons   Area of Help

_____   _____

_____   _____

_____   _____

_____   _____

_____   _____

_____   _____

V. I will reach my goal on:

_____   _____   _____
  (day)   (month)   (year)

P.S. I will ask the following people to follow up on my progress:

_____

_____

_____

_____

_____

_____

5

How to Get the Job You Want

Now that you have determined what your work needs are and identified the kinds of jobs that appeal to you, how can you successfully approach the potential employers on your list? The methods you will use to persuade one of them to hire you will differ, depending on the type of career choice you have made, but whatever that choice was you'll want to plan your strategy carefully.

If you have concluded that you do not have long-time career ambitions, that instead your primary work need is income, your best bet may be simply to watch the employment ads, contact employment agencies, and visit the employment office of the firms you have identified.

All large companies maintain personnel offices where you can apply. The usual procedure, once you present yourself, is to fill out an application form, which may vary depending on the type of work you are seeking. It will elicit information about your education, training, and previous work experience. If you have had a number of previous employers, you may have trouble remembering dates, so it's a good idea to take a chronology of your work experience with you. When you have completed the

61

application, you will probably be interviewed briefly by a personnel department employee who has been trained to "size you up" quickly.

If you pass this first "screening" and there's a job open that you're qualified for, you may then be referred to the appropriate department head for a further interview. If the department head is impressed, you will probably be asked to return to the personnel office to be scheduled for the physical examination that most large companies require prior to employment. While the personnel counselors await the results of the physical, which may take several days, they'll check with your previous employers, and perhaps with the educational institutions you have listed, to verify that you possess the education and experience that you have claimed. If all the results are positive, you may be offered the job.

If there is no vacancy at the moment, but you have made a good impression on the interviewer, you probably will be told that your application will be kept on file so that you can be called when a vacancy occurs. You will have no way of knowing whether this is a serious possibility, or simply a device used by the company's representative to terminate the interview gracefully. However, even if the interviewer is sincere, you may not be called when a vacancy does occur. Your file will be competing with those of many other applicants, some of whom may have more impressive qualifications. Or, if an equally qualified candidate happens to be in the office on the day the vacancy occurs, he or she may be hired on the spot. It's easier for the company to hire someone who is present and ready to go to work than to search the file for other qualified applicants, and then waste time tracking them down only to discover that they are no longer available or interested. Consequently, if your employment search is an extended one, make periodic follow-up calls to the companies that have your application.

If you choose this direct approach, your principal allies—beyond your personality and skills—will be perseverance and luck. Depending on conditions in the job market, you may have to fill out many applications and pay a lot of carfare before you are fortunate enough to be in the right place at the right time.

Your success will also depend largely on your skill in filling out application forms and in responding to the questions asked of you during your interviews. To the extent that the form permits, try to include in your application information that will set you apart from other applicants.

Job Hunting Strategy for the Career Woman

If you have determined that work has a high priority in your life, and you have decided that you want a lifetime career that offers opportunities for advancement, you will want to proceed with your search in a more deliberate, organized, and orderly fashion. The first step—a crucial one—will be the preparing of a resume.

The importance of an effective resume is apparent when you consider that the larger corporations get as many as two thousand unsolicited resumes every week. These are submitted without invitation, such as a newspaper ad. They are lighting candles in the darkness hoping that one will shine on a potential employer.

As you draft your resume, keep your thoughts fixed on its purpose. Remember, you are making a "cold" approach to the firms you have selected, and your objective is to impress them sufficiently so that they will invite you to be interviewed. Therefore your resume must be persuasive enough to cause it to stand out among the hundreds that are received each week.

There are many theories about resume preparation, and a myriad of books that will tell you how to write one. In my experience, however, none has ever adequately addressed the technique of preparing a resume if you are a woman. This is critical because, while the education, training, and experience of male applicants usually are oriented toward business careers, those of a woman applicant often are not. Unless you are skillful in presenting your qualifications, you may turn off employers—usually male—because your experience does not fit their concept of adequate preparation for a business career. Here are some tips:

First, exclude references to your experience in clerical functions such as typing, filing, etc., unless this is the kind of position you want. The reason is simple. Most men are accustomed to thinking of women only in clerical roles, and do not consider women in these positions to be candidates for larger responsibilities. If your resume includes references to these functions, you may be stereotyped immediately as a clerical type, and excluded from consideration for supervisory or management posts. On the other hand, if you have had experience working in a factory, or at other manual chores, that's great! Include this background because it is experience men can relate to, and it will cause them to view you differently, as a woman who's not afraid to pitch in and get her hands dirty. They will respect you because you are more like them.

If your only past experience has been clerical, your task is to find ways of describing your work that will make it sound more significant. For example, use as many administrative action verbs as possible. Don't list typing as a skill or job responsibility; describe yourself as "responsible for the preparation of documents." Don't say you have experience at collating; you were "responsible for assembling information." If you have been a secretary, describe your duties with action verbs, "handles or channels requests," "coordinates activities of department manager," "maintains contact with outside sources," or "follows up on special projects."

The following resume was prepared by a woman whom I counseled. Not only did it get her in the door for an interview, it won her a responsible position and she is now well on her way to a rewarding business career. I have edited it only slightly to avoid any possibility that her employer might recognize it.

Anyone reading this resume would conclude that this was a candidate with broad and responsible experience; one well worth interviewing. In fact, my friend did have broad and responsible experience, but she had been a secretary all her working life. She was simply clever enough to recognize that to achieve her first objective—an interview—she would have to present herself in the most professional-sounding and businesslike way possible. Because she made her work experience sound important, and wrote in business language, she achieved

RESUME OF

(Your Name)

**IMMEDIATE
OBJECTIVE:**   Position in industrial relations or production management field.

EXPERIENCE: Widget Manufacturing Company
Industrial Relations
Corporate Office - Chicago

Report to the director, labor relations. Responsible for coordinating activities of nine industrial relations department managers. Maintain contact with outside firms for purposes of follow-up on special projects.

**May 1970 -
Present**   Participate in and supervise clerical and administrative duties in connection with labor negotiations. Responsible for assembling materials and information from steel and mining companies for use in negotiations. Have knowledge of activities and policies of the unions in our various company locations, grievance procedures and strategies for resolution of union/management difficulties.

Familiar with plant facilities and their relationship to corporate goals and objectives. Handle or channel to the appropriate departments requests from executives relating to labor relations matters.

Assist in preparation of data for Board of Directors meetings, new incentive program for executives, presentations to the Board and company-wide personnel regarding affirmative action, safety standards and other special programs.

**March 1962 -
April 1970**   Rubber Division   Secretary

Advanced through various secretarial positions in the largest division of the company. Had wide exposure to the complexities of a large corporation through positions in marketing, manufacturing, and the executive disciplines in the Rubber Division.

EDUCATION: Eureka College. Will graduate in June, 1978 with a B.A. degree in business administration. Intend to obtain M.B.A.

PERSONAL: Date of Birth: January 25, 1950
Married, no children
Excellent health
Willing to relocate or travel extensively.

CONTACT: Home address and Telephone Number

REFERENCES: Available on Request

her objective. Had she acknowledged that her total experience was as a secretary, the odds are that she would not even have been invited in the door, or at best, would have been offered another secretarial job.

A second useful tip, unless you enjoy typing resumes, is to describe your career objectives in a cover letter and not in the resume itself. Unless you know exactly what kind of a job you want, and won't consider anything else, you will be applying to several companies for many different types of positions. In many cases, you may be answering ads. Rather than type a new resume to fit each circumstance, simply tailor the cover letter to fit the situation.

But it's always a good idea to identify a specific career objective in your cover letter. If you don't, you'll waste the stamp. No personnel officer, wading through the daily flood of application letters and resumes, is going to waste his time trying to identify a job for you if you don't know what you want yourself. This advice also applies to the error of stating a job objective so broad that it is meaningless. I shudder when I receive a job application that says: "My job objective is to utilize my past experiences and abilities in an area which will allow me growth possibilities," or uses similar language that is equally vague. Impress your prospective employer by being specific about your job interests, because this tells him that you have thought about your interests and skills, that you have sense enough to plan, and that you are serious about your career.

My final tip on resumes is that you emphasize functional areas of responsibility rather than job titles. Recite your experience with administration, supervision, coordination. Describe the functions that you have worked with indirectly—advertising, marketing, systems, etc. Try to present a portrait of an experienced business person who has been exposed to a breadth of activities, and has a well-rounded business background.

After you have composed a resume that satisfies you, put yourself in the role of the Personnel Manager, and consider whether you would be impressed or even interested if you had received the resume as one of a score or more that crossed your desk that day. Would it have prompted you to invite the applicant to your office for an interview? If not, analyze its weaknesses and strengthen it, still looking at it from the point of view of those who will receive it. Remember, it's not necessary to include every detail of your life or career. Don't load the resume with superfluous detail; focus on the impressive highlights.

Remember, too, that this is not a time to be humble. Psychologists have observed that another culturally induced handicap of women is our low sense of self-worth, perhaps because society requires so many of us to work without pay at tasks that don't impart much respect. How many women have you heard say on the TV quiz shows, "I'm just a housewife"? Most women are not good at bragging. You can test that by asking your female friends to write down their strong points. Most of them will have trouble coming up with three or four. Then ask a man the same question. He'll probably write an essay.

The point is important because business careers are rarely built on humility. A humble resume won't help you because the shy, timid, retiring souls start their careers in the shadows and usually remain there, cursing the darkness. Your resume is the candle that will shed light on your attributes, so don't hide it under a bushel. Be positive about yourself. Exude confidence, because that's a major virtue in business circles.

You can overdo it, of course. I recently saw the resume of a woman who did. She included the heading "Personal Appearance" and beneath it noted, "Very attractive." It's one thing to confidently identify your skills and quite another to brag.

Should a Professional Prepare Your Resume?

It's important that your resume have a professional appearance. If you don't have access to a good typewriter and the skill to operate it, it may be wise to have your resume typed by a professional. I don't believe it is necessary to have a resume professionally printed; in fact, with some employers a printed resume may produce a negative reaction. It may imply to them that you are so lacking in confidence that you expect to canvass the universe before you find someone willing to employ you. Your resume should, however, be neat, legible, and free of grammatical, spelling, and typographical errors. That may seem to you an obvious requirement, but you would be astounded by the number of resumes received by employers that are submitted in illegible longhand, full of misspelled words, bad grammar, and errors in punctuation. The inevitable conclusion of the employer who gets one of these is that anyone so careless in her efforts to get a job will probably be even sloppier about her work when she begins to perform it.

Who Should Get Your Resume?

If you want to find the best job that's out there, you'll work hard to maximize the odds so that they're in your favor. The more people who see your resume the better the chances that you will be invited for several interviews, and have the opportunity to pick and choose among a number of offers. You may wish to send your resume to a number of people in the same company, if it is one that is particularly attractive to you. It could, for example, go to the personnel department, the president of the company, and to the executive responsible for the area of corporate activity in which you are interested. If it doesn't appeal to one of them it may arouse the interest of another.

You can also enhance your prospects of finding the best job available by sending your resume to others who are not themselves prospective employers. Don't, for example, overlook sending copies to your friends who know you and your talents well. They may know of openings, or have well-placed acquaintances who do. If you are already employed and seeking a management level job, consider sending copies of your resume to executive search firms, employment agencies, and counseling groups. They may have a current job order which matches your qualifications.

Should You Try to Make Your Resume Look Different?

You want your resume to stand out among the others, but the use of artificial devices to accomplish this is generally not a good idea. It is your qualifications you want to highlight, not typographical wizardry, or other gimmicks to separate your resume from the pile. I have seen many resumes that were ingeniously unique, but also so drastically different from the accustomed format that they turned the recipient off, not on.

You will be wise to remember that business is basically conservative, and that frivolous devices may create an impression contrary to the one you want to encourage. The most important considerations are neatness, accuracy, and a description of your talents, skills, and experience that will cause the reader to conclude that you could become a valued and productive employee of the firm.

Should You Include Your Picture?

Visual impressions are important, and if you believe that your appearance will be an asset in your search for employment, it may help to include a photograph. If you do, however, be sure it's a good one. Don't send amateur snapshots, or arty poses in which you look like a photographer's model rather than a businesswoman. The personnel manager may be the type who closes his office door during the lunch hour so he can admire the woman in the centerfold of *Playboy*, but he doesn't call her up after lunch to invite her to work for his company. Your photo should portray you as an attractive, but serious and businesslike woman who looks like she would be an excellent candidate for a business career.

How Long Should Your Resume Be?

Unless you have had very extensive work experience which simply must be included, you should try to hold your resume to a single page. If it is essential that it be longer, the best technique is to summarize your total experience on the first page, and then use the second page to go into greater detail. Never forget that personnel officers are busy people who are flooded with paper. Some of them simply won't bother to wade through a resume that goes on forever.

If your first attempt runs several pages in length, go through it carefully and edit out all but the most essential details. You will probably find that you can reduce it to one page without sacrificing anything crucial, and at the same time give it a great deal more punch. I have seen resumes of corporate presidents who wanted to change companies after twenty-five or more years in the business world and managed to put their salient career details on a single page.

What About References?

Depending on the level of position you want, there may be a point at which you will be asked to submit references other than those identified in your resume as former employers. These might include business acquaintances, clergymen, educators who know you well, and bankers and others familiar with your financial and credit status. Include in your resume the phrase, "References on request," and have in mind the names of those you will supply if asked to do so. It is generally pointless, however, to include references in the resume itself unless you can provide names of people whose stature is so well-recognized that your credibility will be enhanced by association with them. If prominent businessmen, educators, or political figures are numbered among your friends, include them as references by all means.

What Should Go in the Cover Letter?

Just as your resume is intended to generate an interview, the cover letter that accompanies it should be framed to induce the recipient to read your resume. It should suggest that your application is more than a shot in the dark; that you have applied to each company that receives it because you're genuinely interested in working for them. If there are aspects of your experience that make you particularly well qualified to contribute to a prospective employer, highlight them in as few words as possible. Finally, as suggested earlier, be specific about your career objective and your reasons for choosing it. Your purpose is to appear sincere, confident, conscientious, and highly motivated to pursue a career with the firm you have approached.

What's Next?

Okay, you've written a concise, thoughtful resume that presents your best face to the world. This neatly typed document, along with a persuasive cover letter, has been sent to the corporations on your most-wanted list and your fate is now in the hands of the gods and the U. S. Postal Service. Or is it?

The answer is "no." You've fired the opening salvo in your battle for a responsible niche in the man's world of business, but you're not going to hibernate in the barracks while you wait to learn whether any of those missiles find their mark. There are some other weapons in your arsenal, and now is the time to put them to work.

Talk with Your Friends

An astonishing percentage of corporate positions are filled by referrals from present employees of the company. While you await the results of your barrage of resumes, you can profitably use the time to seek help from friends who are already employed in business, or may have knowledge of openings in your field of interest. The corporate grapevine buzzes with information about existing or potential vacancies and, in some companies, job openings are posted to permit present employees to apply. Thus some of your friends may be aware of openings in their firm that are suitable for you.

If so, tell them you would like to submit your resume to the company's personnel office, with a cover letter indicating that they mentioned the position to you. Or, as an alternative, ask them to submit your resume to the personnel department—or to the executive who has the authority to fill the vacant position. This gives you a distinct edge over other applicants who submit their resumes "cold." First, you are applying for a vacancy that you know exists, so you can't be put off with a statement that nothing is available. Second, because you know the precise job that is available, you can draft a cover letter that emphasizes your qualifications for that specific position. Finally, you have an ally who is already employed by the company who can be your advocate and reassure the hiring executive about your qualifications and abilities.

A Little "Pull" Can Also Help

If you know a well-placed executive in one of the companies on your list, don't hesitate to utilize that connection. In your search for employment, you are competing with many others, and your objective is to make your talents stand out over theirs. While your friend in the executive suite may not be willing to exercise influence to see that you are employed, he or she can see that your application receives full consideration, and this association in itself may influence employment representatives in making their decision. "Pull" probably won't get the job for you if you don't deserve it, but it may tip the scales if you are one among several who do.

One thing is certain: An executive with power in a company can assure that you are granted an interview. However, be aware that the interview may be granted as a courtesy even if there are no openings for which you are qualified. Don't get your hopes too high if you used influence to obtain an interview, because it may be a courtesy situation in which no one has any real intention of putting you on the payroll.

Private Employment Agencies

Where the more desirable and responsible jobs are concerned, most employment agencies these days are compensated by the employer when they help fill a vacancy. The advantage of registering with an employment agency is access to the known vacancies they have on file. The disadvantage is that they may waste a great deal of your time by sending you on interviews for positions that don't really interest you, or firms whose working conditions may not be ideal. To the agency you are a commodity, and they can make money only when they place you. Consequently, they may run you ragged on interviews for jobs that don't really suit your work needs, in the hope that you may, in desperation, accept one of them.

You can avoid wasting your time if you screen the jobs they try to send you out on. Ask them to be very specific about the job before you go or you may find that you have wasted a morning talking to a company you don't like about a job in which you have no interest. The same precaution is advisable if you register with one of the publicly funded employment agencies, for their procedures are essentially the same as the private employment services, except that they receive no fee.

School Placement Services

The schools you attended, whether high school, vocational school, or college, probably maintain placement offices. Most students are aware of these services prior to graduation, and you may have utilized one when you completed your education.

Many job-seekers forget, however, that these services are also available to alumni. Don't overlook the possibility that your school's placement service may have knowledge of existing vacancies for which you are suited, perhaps even with one of the companies that is on your list.

Situation Wanted Advertising

If you are already on your way toward a career in a specialized profession, there may be trade publications and professional journals in which you can advertise your availability at a relatively nominal charge. In many cities, the Sunday newspapers also offer this opportunity, although probably at a higher cost. If you feel you can afford it, you might try this avenue as a backup for your other efforts.

Executive Search Firms

Many corporations retain consulting firms to assist them in locating qualified personnel, usually at the middle management or executive level. More familiarly known as "headhunters," their procedure is exactly what that title implies; they are paid by the company to find people for "hard to fill" positions. They may not maintain a file of job applicants, but instead conduct searches as specific personnel needs are presented to them by their clients. However, if you are already qualified for a middle management spot, you have nothing to lose by sending your resume to some of them, and who knows? Lightning may strike.

Be wary of the firms that identify themselves as executive search firms but survive largely on fees paid to them by job-seekers for counseling, resume preparation, etc. The odds are that firms which rely primarily on income from applicants rather than from employers probably don't have many jobs to offer.

Special Women's Counseling Groups

Federal equal employment pressures and increased opportunities for women have spawned a number of groups across the country that specialize in counseling and placing women in business careers. One of the best-known is a New York group called Catalyst. This group will supply you with a form on which you list your qualifications, job interests, salary expectations, areas of geographical interest, educational background, and other pertinent details. This information is then fed into its computer, which produces a listing that is circulated to the companies that subscribe to their service. The listing does not give your name, but any company that is interested in you and your qualifications can contact Catalyst so that an interview can be arranged.

In addition to Catalyst, there are some other groups—Flexible Careers, in Chicago, for example—which function as counseling services and placement agencies for women. They offer another tool you can use in your search for prospective employers.

Hang on to Your Present Job

If there is a classic axiom of job-hunting it is this: *The best time to find a job is when you've already got one.* Many women, frustrated in their existing situation, decide to quit before they have uncovered a more desirable alternative. It is a mistake, because you have a psychological advantage over a prospective employer if you are not desperately in need of employment, and a disadvantage if you are. Further, if you quit your job, prospective employers may have doubts about whether you really quit or got fired. It is difficult for most personnel representatives to comprehend giving up one job without having another. Even if they believe you when you tell them you resigned, they probably will question your judgment for having taken so desperate a gamble. These suspicions would not apply, of course, if you have interrupted your work experience to return to college or raise a family and are now returning to the work force.

Even if your current position is almost unbearable, hang onto it until you find something better. Admittedly, your search may be hampered by the requirements of your present job, but it is better to endure this handicap than invite the greater obstacle that unemployment would be in the eyes of a prospective employer.

Time to Follow Up

A week has passed since your list of prospective employers received your resume. You have used this period to your advantage, but now it's time to follow up on your basic strategy. Telephone or visit the personnel officers or other executives to whom you submitted your resume. Stress your eagerness to work for their particular company and respectfully request an interview. Be very direct and businesslike; assertive, but not aggressive. Request an appointment at a specific time that is convenient for them.

Follow-up is necessary because your application may be submerged in the flood of resumes that most companies receive each week. More important, however, is the fact that your follow-up call indicates a genuine interest in the company, and demonstrates a degree of initiative and assertiveness that will be regarded as desirable traits by most of those who work in the corporate world.

The Interview: How to Get a Job Offer

Hopefully, the time and effort you have expended in contacting prospective employers will produce opportunities for interviews. But be sure to prepare yourself before you go to an interview. Determine the job parameters that are important to you. Be prepared to discuss your salary requirements, your willingness to relocate and where, your attitude toward career and family alternatives, your work needs and objectives. You will want to impress the interviewer with the fact that you are serious about your business career and have thought about it carefully.

Your Image Will Be Important

Unless you're hoping to become a Playboy bunny, the rules of the game are basically the same for any job at any level in the business world. You should look and act like a business woman. The male employers whom you must impress will react more positively if you are dressed conservatively, wear your hair in a neat style, and apply your makeup with discretion. If you deviate too much from the way business people look and expect other business people to look, you will reduce your chances of being offered the job you want.

You may like "in" attire and own a flamboyant wardrobe. Enjoy it when you are away from the job, but dress the business role when you appear for your job interviews. I couldn't begin to count the number of times I have seen well-qualified women sacrifice job opportunities because their inappropriate dress turned off the department manager before he had the chance to learn what they could do. Looking like a business woman can even overcome deficiencies in skills and experience. During my career, I have seen many women hired whose qualifications weren't outstanding, but who did "look the part" of a business woman. Consider my friend Joanne, a secretary, who decided she wanted to move up into management. Curious about why some employees made it while others didn't, she was clever enough to observe that, without exception, management people in her company carried attaché cases to and from the office.

Joanne decided to test this status symbol. She bought and began carrying an olive green attaché case. She did nothing to change her behavior except carry the case whenever she left the office each day. Within three weeks she had been offered a supervisory position. Sounds ridiculous, doesn't it? It may be, but what it tells you about the power of suggestion is well worth learning. If you look like an executive, there is a good chance that you will be treated like one. That's why, when you report for an interview, it is so critical that you look the part.

When to Arrive for Your Interview

Unlike some social situations, there is no such thing as being "fashionably late" where job interviews are concerned. On the contrary, I recommend that you arrive fifteen minutes before the appointed time. This will give you a chance to relax, check your appearance, and be prepared to present a cool, confident, "put-together" image, rather than appearing breathless and distraught. It is important that you appear confident, calm, and collected, and that you know it.

It is also important to remember that in many cases your interview may actually be in progress the moment you walk into the reception area. Some receptionists are expected to observe your behavior while you wait and to give feedback to the person who interviews you. If you make a bad impression on the receptionist, it could cost you the job. So be pleasant to her, and watch your behavior in her presence so that she is encouraged to become an ally, not a detractor.

Be Aware of Your Actions

Watch your body language, which often communicates more effectively than words. You will undoubtedly be nervous, particularly in your early interview experiences, but do your best to collect yourself and appear confident and relaxed. Avoid any mannerism that may reinforce the female stereotype; remember, you are trying to make the interviewer believe that you have the personality and qualities that lead to success in business.

Try to remember to keep your hands below your waist. Don't play with your hair or face, or fidget with your purse. This may sound like frivolous advice, but it is incredible how many of us do these things instinctively when we are nervous. Appear pleasant but serious, but don't be afraid to smile if there is something to smile about. Businessmen may be conservative, but they know that a sense of humor at the right moment can be invaluable.

When you greet your interviewer be friendly and assertive; offer a firm handshake. Create the impression from the outset that you are fully prepared to deal with this situation, thus demonstrating your capacity to handle the challenges of the position you are seeking.

What If You Are Subjected to Illegal Questions?

Antidiscrimination laws prohibit the asking of some personal questions; for example questions about whether you plan to have children, how you are going to get to work, or the birth control method you use. Some women's counseling services recommend that if such questions are asked you immediately confront the interviewer with the fact that he doesn't have the right to ask that question.

Assuredly, this kind of response will make you feel better about yourself as a woman, and it may shake up the man who asked the question, but it isn't apt to help you get the job. In fact, if you confront a male interviewer this way, he will probably label you a potential trouble-maker and reject your application. Always keep in mind that your objective during the interview is to get a job offer. Conduct yourself in a manner that will achieve this objective.

Once you have the offer in hand, you can consider how you should respond to illegal questioning. You will probably want to weigh the extent to which it may indicate the company's position on equal employment opportunity. You may even conclude that you don't want to work for a company that pries into your birth control methods before offering you a job. In lieu of confrontation during the interview, you can then consider whether you want to report your experience to the proper authorities.

What to Emphasize During Your Interview

Don't approach your interview expecting to be cross-examined. The purpose of the interview is to elicit information about you, of course, and you should respond readily and convincingly to the questions that are asked. But remember, this is also your opportunity to volunteer information about yourself, not revealed by the questioning, that you think will help you get the offer. Most important, it is your opportunity to ask some questions yourself, to determine whether the job in question suits your needs.

This is important, not only to help you make the right career choice, but also because it will demonstrate to the interviewer that you are serious about your career—and intelligent enough to want to avoid a career choice that would fail to satisfy your needs or those of your employer.

Small Talk

Most interviewers will open the conversation with small talk—about the weather, a recent news event, or perhaps an inquiry about whether you had difficulty finding the office. Be prepared with some small talk of your own, so there aren't any awkward silences, but don't prolong it with an extended dissertation on one of the subjects the interviewer may raise. The interviewer is simply trying to put you at ease while forming a first impression of you. If you're observant you'll know when he or she is ready to get down to the business at hand.

Everything Means Something

Don't respond thoughtlessly to any question, however irrelevant or trivial it may seem. Your every word and reaction is being noted and will form part of the total impression that you leave. Sometimes a thoughtless answer to a seemingly insignificant question may be the remark that costs you the job. I have in mind a high potential applicant whom I referred to Walter, a friend who is an employment manager for a major corporation. The applicant was currently working in New York City, but had her heart set on returning to the Midwest.

During the interview, Walter casually asked her how she liked New York. "I hate it," she replied, launching into a five minute diatribe about the evils of the Big Apple. When she finished her attack on New York, in Walter's mind, the interview was over. He had been prepared to offer an exceptional opportunity, but he feared she would accept any job just to get out of New York— even one that might not hold her interest for long.

The point is that anything you say may have meaning to the interviewer that wasn't apparent in the question. Consider your replies carefully and avoid volunteering "far out" opinions that may alienate the person on the other side of the desk.

Questions About Your Future

Most interviewers will try to draw you out about your career objectives and other goals in life, now and in the more distant future. It is important to them to know whether you are career-oriented and thus a prospect for lifetime employment, or desirous of combining a family with your career. Your task is to demonstrate that you have thought a great deal about your future and that you do have a plan. This shows good business sense because planning is an important aspect of business. If your goal is supervision and ultimately management, it also presents an opportunity to indicate that you want a situation where you can progress upward in your career.

Remember, if your interviewer is a man, the odds are heavy that he may hold the stereotyped view that women lack commitment to our jobs. This is an opportunity to demonstrate by your response that such a stereotype is not descriptive of you.

Do You Plan to Have a Family?

Although this question is illegal, it almost certainly will be asked in one or more of your interviews. Your reaction could be an angry one, which could help to reinforce the preconceived notion of a male interviewer that you, "like other women," are too emotional. You may find it easier to bite your tongue and restrain your anger if you recognize why the question is asked. Companies fear investing large sums in training women who will suddenly announce that they are pregnant just about the time they become fully productive on the job. You and I know that this possibility doesn't justify penalizing all women simply because some may quit to have babies. Men don't have babies, but they quit, too. Deal with this question by remembering that you are under no obligation to disclose personal facts in response to an illegal question. Sidestep the question by responding with an enthusiastic affirmation of your commitment to a business career.

Why Do You Want to Work?

This question, coming from a man, usually means that another stereotype has raised its ugly head. Many men are so convinced that for women marriage is the most important goal that they can't understand why you would work instead of opting for marriage. They assume that you are doing it for a lark, perhaps to earn some pin money, but that before long you'll disappear into the home and arms of some "good provider" like themselves. It is important to convince the interviewer that you are work-oriented, that your major satisfaction in life will come from pursuing a successful business career. Make it clear that you are motivated by the challenges, the sense of achievement, and many of the same reasons that motivate him. It may also be wise to make it clear that you do have financial needs as well as personal ambitions that compel you to opt for a business career.

Will You Travel and/or Relocate?

If asked about travel or relocation, give an honest response that demonstrates again that you have considered your career thoughtfully and identified the parameters within which you choose to work. If you are willing to travel and relocate, you will, of course, say so. If you are not, you should also say so, but if this is a temporary situation, occasioned by some need such as the responsibility for an elderly relative, make that clear too. Deception would be pointless, because if you have indicated a willingness to move and then refuse a promotion because relocation is required, your hopes for upward progress will come to an abrupt and certain end.

How Do You Feel about Working with Men?

If you have had prior experience in a male-dominated work environment, describe it and indicate that your relationships with your male co-workers were positive. If you have successfully supervised males, or headed a social organization that included males among its members, by all means say so. Make it clear that you are capable of relating to men on a platonic basis, so that you will disabuse the interviewer of any stereotypes he as a male may have about *that*. Make it clear without saying so directly that, while you have not taken a vow of celibacy, you reserve your personal relationships with men to your nonbusiness environment.

What Do You Have to Offer This Company?

This is the time to pull out all the stops. What you are really being asked is why you should be chosen for this position in preference to all the other applicants—all of whom may be men. Do some homework before you go on your first interview and have your reply to this one carefully prepared in advance. You want to be as comprehensive, convincing, and articulate as possible. Your response will highlight your experience, your education, your skills, your accomplishments not only in business but in your private life. Perhaps you have demonstrated leadership ability in school or in social organizations. If so, point it out. Finally, if the job is one to which you, as a woman, can bring talents, insights, or skills they won't get from a man, bear down hard on them. If the interviewer is a man, that possibility may never have crossed his mind. Reach for the qualities that may set you apart from others, male and female, who are also seeking the job.

"Tell Me about Your Background"

The interviewer has already read your resume or job application, so it is not really repetitive biographical detail that he or she seeks. You are being given an opportunity to demonstrate how succinct and articulate you can be in presenting yourself to a stranger. This will reveal how well you will do, if hired, in representing the company, or in dealing with subordinates, peers, and supervisors.

Don't get into your vital statistics. The interviewer already has those. Instead, expand on the information contained in your resume, elaborating on the background and experience that will have the most value in your business career. If you have had no full-time experience, emphasize part-time employment, or non-business experience and training or education that has helped you to understand the world of work. This is another reply that you should carefully prepare in advance, so that you won't fumble your response because you have been caught off guard.

Why Do You Want This Job?

You certainly don't reply that you haven't eaten all week, or baby needs a pair of shoes, or you can't find anything else. The strongest response is one that suggests that you have considered the company and the job it offers and are convinced that you can make an important contribution to the company and have the opportunity for personal growth. The question was asked because the interviewer is still trying to find out what you can do for the company, and how well you will do it. You want to stimulate a positive reaction by providing assurance that you have matched your skills to the job he has to offer and are convinced that it is one that you can perform in the best interests of the company, as well as your own.

Why Are You Leaving Your Present Job?

Handle this one with discretion, because it may be crucial. The worst response you can make is one that indicates dissatisfaction, or is critical of your present employer. The interviewer has no way of knowing who's right and who's wrong, and his inevitable inclination may be to side with your employer. Even if you're leaving because your present boss is a male chauvinist S. O. B., don't say so. A good general rule is never to say anthing derogatory about a former employer or supervisor. The interviewer may visualize you, in some future interview, saying the same sort of things about him.

A far better approach in responding to this question is to assert that your job changes in the past have been planned to help you meet your career objectives. If you wish, you may indicate that your growth potential in your present position is limited and explain why. You may have a host of other legitimate, positive reasons for wanting to change jobs, and if so, don't hesitate to talk about them. The best approach of all is to indicate your belief that your opportunities to learn and grow will be enhanced in a position with the company to which you are applying.

As with every other question you were asked, try to provide a response that will emphasize that you are career-minded and willing to put forth the effort and make the sacrifices that are essential to a successful business career.

What to Say If You Have Been Fired

If the interviewer is aware that you were discharged from your previous job, don't be evasive or dishonest in discussing it. Chances are he can determine with one phone call what the reasons were. Confront the issue in a direct manner, giving the basic reason for the termination without elaborating on the details.

The fact that you have been dismissed from a job is certainly not helpful, but neither is it an insurmountable obstacle. Business is based on conflict and competition, and most business people—probably including your interviewer—will recognize that all conflicts cannot be resolved. You aren't the first person that has lost a job, nor the first discharged applicant the interviewer has hired. Explain the situation in its best possible light, assuming as much responsibility for the situation as is appropriate and without blaming anyone for what happened. Calm, rational handling of a difficult situation may actually improve your image in the interviewer's eyes.

What Salary Do You Require?

Yes, sooner or later you do have to get to the bottom line, and when you do, be prepared for it. It is not unusual for job applicants to offer the weakest response there is: "What does the job pay?" If you appear unaware of the going rate, and of your own worth, the answer will probably be, "Not very much."

You have several options in responding to this question, and your choice should be determined by how badly you want the job. One tactic is to set a high figure with the thought that it's the basis for negotiation, and you are prepared to come down a bit. Another is to state a figure and make it clear that there is no room for negotiation. This is a response you should make only if this is truly the minimum you will accept, but if you make it be prepared for the possibility that you won't get the job because the company's salary structure won't go that high. In most companies, every salary is part of an overall wage scale. The whole structure may be threatened if they deviate from it too much in filling one particular job.

The salary question is one that deserves some advance research. If you really want the job you don't want to overprice your services and lose the opportunity, nor do you want to underprice them and lose the money. Your objective is to be offered a starting salary that is the maximum you can expect to obtain under the circumstances. Remember, every dollar you can get in starting salary is one you won't have to wait for future increases to earn.

You can handle this problem with confidence if you have the facts. Try to determine before the interview the going rate in this industry for the type of position which is involved. Through contacts within the company, you may even be able to determine precisely what the normal salary range is for the position in question. If you can respond with a figure that is adequate for you and in the ball park for the company, you will indicate knowledge of the company and confidence in yourself. If you are hesitant and unsure, you will suggest ignorance of the market, and a lack of confidence in your ability to make a significant contribution to your prospective employer.

Having stated the figure, be prepared for the next question: "You're asking for a lot of money. Why do you think you're worth it?" This gives you another opportunity to recite your qualifications—and also to indicate your awareness of what the market is for someone who has them.

The interviewer's alternative response to your salary request may be a statement that the job doesn't pay that much. Your recourse then is to make a comment that will encourage him to make an offer which you can accept or reject, as you choose.

What To Do If The Job Is Offered

If the position you are seeking is at a higher level, it is unusual for a job offer to be made on the spot. Normally, the personnel department will want to do reference checks with previous employers and verify the educational credentials that you have claimed. Yet sometimes it does happen. If so, don't accept the job out of hand. Tell the interviewer that you want to consider it among other options, leaving him the impression that he has made a wise choice because your services are in demand. When you accept it, that impression may further your progress in the job.

What Questions Should You Ask?

It is best, when you report for an interview, to have some knowledge of the company that is involved. If it is a manufacturing firm, for example, have some knowledge of its products. Obtain a copy of the firm's annual report and study its financial condition, sales volume, and other pertinent details about its operations. Familiarize yourself with the top executives who manage the company.

This preparation will enable you to ask intelligent questions about the company while impressing the interviewer with your diligence and your apparent interest in the job. Ask questions about the prospective future of the firm, about opportunities for advancement, about the career ladder on which you hope to make upward progress. Inquire about training opportunities and educational programs that will enable you to enhance your value to the firm.

Eventually, you will also want to ask about employee benefits—insurance plans, vacations, retirement programs, profit-sharing plans, and the like—but save these questions and ask them after you have been offered the job, if information about them is not volunteered at that time. Many interviewers will be turned off if you appear to be preoccupied with benefits, rather than the content and opportunities afforded by the job.

What to Bring to an Interview

Depending on the nature of the job, and what you are prepared to supply, you may want to bring documents to the interview that will enhance your credibility. These could be letters of reference from people of stature who know you and your qualifications. They could be articles that have been written about you, articles you have written for professional journals, or samples of your previous work. The technical materials may not be of interest to the interviewer if he is a personnel department employee because he probably will not be a specialist in your field. However, they may be of value when you are interviewed by the department head for whom you actually will work.

Interviewing for Jobs in Sales, Plant Supervision, and Skilled Trades

Although the information in the previous pages is directed primarily toward the career-oriented woman, much of it has application to those who want to improve their work situation without actually pointing toward managerial responsibility. Let's look now at interviews in the three areas I have identified which offer opportunities for those without specific experience, training, and skills. They were, you remember, sales, production or plant supervision, and crafts and skilled trades.

If you are an inexperienced woman applying for a position in sales, the interviewer will be looking for an outgoing and assertive personality. The company will be searching for someone whose appearance and behavior will represent the corporation well in the outside world. The interviewer will observe whether you make direct eye contact or do not. Failure to make direct eye contact may give you a shifty appearance. He will ask questions that will help him determine your ability to communicate information and ideas affectively and to demonstrate your ability to think on your feet. He will try to determine, through subtle questioning, whether you are a self-starter who can be expected to keep your nose to the grindstone in a situation where you are allowed to work independently. Prepare in advance for your interview, keeping these concerns of the interviewer in mind.

The primary interest of the interviewer, if you are applying for a job in plant supervision, will be evidence of leadership ability. He will want someone who is able to communicate well, who is straightforward in her dealings with others. A large part of supervision is your ability to communicate thoughts and directions clearly, sometimes to unskilled employees who may not match your intellectual capacity, and this, too, will concern the person who interviews you.

Appearance and manner are also important. Plant situations tend to be very informal, so you should not appear for your interview looking as though you had just stepped out of Bonwit Teller or Neiman-Marcus. Dress neatly and conservatively. It is also important that you appear calm and relaxed during your interview, for part of your job will involve counseling and disciplining employees, a role that requires firmness, strength of character, and emotional stability.

When interviewing for an apprentice position or a job in a skilled trade, try to present a bright, alert image, but dress on the conservative and informal side. You want to try to look the part you are seeking, to offset the stereotype that these are not really jobs for women. In your discussion, stress your reasons for being interested in a nontraditional position for a woman. Make it clear that your interest is a well thought out, serious one, not a whim. If you have samples of work you have done in the trade that interests you, and you don't need a truck to move them, bring them along. They may lend credibility to your talents in your field of interest.

How to Decide Among Job Offers

It's certainly not a fate worse than death, but you may find yourself perplexed if you have to decide among several job offers. Don't let it throw you. Go back to your analysis of work needs and chart them again, in relation to the specific jobs that have been offered. Chances are the results will make the choice for you.

There are, however, some other specifics you should keep in mind in making your choice. Money is important to all of us, of course, but don't let it tempt you to forsake your other work needs. Remember, for example, that if you accept a position that pays well initially, but does nothing to increase your skills so, you can grow on the job, your earning potential may quickly plateau. Sometimes it pays to settle for less money now, in order to earn considerably more later. Weigh all the factors that concern you before you finally accept a job.

6

Personal Growth Techniques That Win a Competitive Edge

As I said at the outset, a major aspect of developing a successful work life is learning the rules of the game. Next we need to learn the emotional behavior that will help us to accomplish our work goals.

We are all familiar with being in the midst of an argument and hearing a little voice in our heads warn, "Don't get mad and don't shout," but we do it anyway. It's almost as though our emotional reaction is beyond our control and impossible to stop. It's not, of course—it's really a case of having established a strong habit pattern that is hard to break.

Although women are stereotyped as being "too emotional," we all know that both men and women have emotions. They are a part of being human. The difference is in the way men and women control and channel their emotions while they are playing the business game. For example, when we as women are upset, or sad, or hurt, our rearing has probably allowed us to cry. Yet, because business is a man's game and they generally don't cry, tears are also seen as inappropriate behavior for businesswomen.

Women tend not to be well trained to deal with conflict situations either; many of us, for example, find it difficult to work effectively with those we don't like. Yet many of these situations are accepted conditions in the business game.

It is important to learn and use appropriate behavior patterns in business, not only to make our work life more pleasant, but to gain the support of those with the power to determine our success or failure—the businessmen.

The personal growth techniques that follow provide a basis for handling most of the conflict situations in your business life. You will find as you learn to use them that you will begin to feel generally in much better control of your life. Most of them will lead to increased self-confidence, not only at work, but in other activities as well.

These personal growth skills will be effective in direct proportion to the practice you give them. What you are trying to do is develop different and better ways of dealing with life situations than you have in the past. You need to practice the new methods until they become natural and you overcome your undesirable habit patterns.

Why Relaxation Is Important

Let's begin with a characteristic common to most successful men and women—the ability to relax at will when exposed to demanding and stressful situations. They don't risk letting themselves get so uptight that they respond hastily, thoughtlessly, emotionally, or irrationally. Developing the ability to relax will provide the foundation for the other techniques and strategies that you will learn in the pages that follow. Your mastery of the techniques of relaxation will also help you to deal with the physical demands that the business world imposes on successful people and to avoid the stress-related illnesses that a highly competitive environment inflicts on many executives. Relaxation is also a way of dealing with the emotional stereotypes that men apply to all women. Let's face it: Most of us do respond more emotionally to difficult situations than men do because we have been trained since childhood to respond that way. That's okay in our personal lives, but it doesn't help in business. Learning to relax can dispose of this syndrome.

Consider for a moment the fact that the mind and body function in close harmony with each other. Tension is a symptom of an emotional response to a stressful situation. If we learn to relax at will in moments of stress, it is virtually impossible for us to become highly emotional about our problems.

Tension control and relaxation should also be regarded as a "must" in business if one of our most valuable assets—our energy—is to be conserved. If we let the competitive pressures of business make us tense, it diminishes our accomplishment, wastes our energy, and may injure our health. Relaxation skills will increase productivity, diminish sensitivity to criticism, help us think clearly so that we can make sound decisions, make better use of time, lessen anxiety, promote a more positive attitude, and decrease fatigue. All of these benefits have been demonstrated in research and experience with tension control.

A Workable, Effective Relaxation Technique

I've already led you through a few intellectual exercises. Now, I'm going to give you some instructions that will teach you physical relaxation. This technique is one that can be used in a variety of body positions—most often used in a prone position—but you're going to learn to do it while sitting down. Why? Because you'll want to use it at the office and it won't help your business image if you're found lying on the floor!

Sit well back in the chair so that your body is fully supported. If you choose to put your legs up on another chair or a higher object, make sure that the small of your back is adequately supported.

Now, begin by breathing in and tightening the muscles all over your body. Be aware of how your body feels in this very tense state. Then exhale and totally let go. Try to eliminate the tension from every muscle in your body. Repeat the process, and again be aware, first, of the tension and then of how your relaxed body feels.

Next, take two or three long, calm, easy breaths, letting your abdominal muscles relax and rise as you do so. Then go back to your ordinary breathing. Close your eyes and focus your thoughts on each part of your body, starting with the muscles of your face. Let your face relax so that your jaw sags and you are aware that your teeth are not tightly together. Now concentrate on relaxing the muscles of your forehead so it becomes smooth and feels tranquil. Be aware of how this state feels. Make sure that none of the muscles in your face are contracted and that your face is without expression.

Now be aware of your neck muscles and how they feel. If there is some tension, try to relax some more. Turn your head from side to side so that you feel the tension and then the comfort as the muscle tension subsides. Next, concentrate on your legs. Check to make sure that your toes are still and your ankles relaxed. Let the floor take the whole weight of your legs so that the muscles become totally relaxed.

Now turn your attention to your arms. Make every muscle, from fingers to shoulders, let go. Your hands will drop and your arms collapse on the arms of your chair. Be aware of your shoulders and let the tension go so that your muscles stop contracting.

Be aware now of the sensation as every muscle in your body becomes limp. Enjoy the feeling as your whole body relaxes. Stop concentrating on its individual parts and be aware of your total body condition. You should feel as though you were sinking through the chair. Every muscle is relaxed and you feel peaceful and comfortable. Your mind is free of everything except the wonderful sensation of total peace.

Stay in this position for a few minutes, remaining aware of the feeling. If you find that your mind has become busy and active again, recheck your body to find where your muscles have contracted. Check your toes, ankles, legs, abdomen, fingers, arms, shoulders, neck, and face and then make yourself aware of the allover sensation. Enjoy again the tranquility that comes when your muscles are relaxed.

You'll find that in this completely relaxed state your mind no longer hassles with problems. Like a parked car, it idles effortlessly and when the relaxation session is over you will feel refreshed and alert. Upon completion of the exercise, get up slowly or you may feel light-headed. Many people use it as a very effective way of putting themselves to sleep. As your skill with this technique increases, be sure you don't let it put you to sleep at the office.

If you practice this technique regularly and take it seriously, you will find that you gradually become able to relax more quickly and for longer periods of time. Eventually, you will find your body sinking into this relaxed state on command. You will be able to call on the technique whenever you are uptight or distressed and quickly become alert, refreshed, and composed. If you practice it often enough it will become a natural response pattern, not something you have to "do."

Emotional Rehearsal Technique

Emotional responses are one of the most discussed and until recently the least understood of all human behaviors. In the last several years, techniques have been developed that allow us to channel our emotions in directions that are constructive rather than destructive. The examples given here were developed specifically for business application, after extensive clinical research.

Dr. David Graham of the University of Wisconsin, a pioneer researcher in the area of human emotions, reports that emotions are physiologic responses to our perceptions of ourselves in relation to the outside world.

Our emotional reactions usually stem from what we believe to be true about something. For example, let's say you are walking along the sidewalk and someone runs into you. Your instinctive emotional reaction will be anger toward the clumsy lout who bumped you, but when you turn to look at that person and discover that he is blind, your angry emotional reaction gives way instantly to one of sympathy and compassion.

This example demonstrates that it is often not the precise act or event that produces our emotional responses but what we *believe* about the act or event. You weren't angry because someone bumped into you but because of your belief about the kind of person who would bump into you. Were this not the case, you would have continued to be angry even after you perceived that the man was blind.

You can see that it is the assumptions we make that disturb or annoy us. We react emotionally to our perceptions of reality based on our belief of what we think reality is.

Women in business today must be extremely aware of their

emotional matrix, particularly as they are subjected to the stresses and conflicts involved in dealing with the hassles of the business world. It is very easy for us to feel a lack of confidence or become depressed or respond inappropriately to perceived actions and events that don't really mean what we believe them to mean. To avoid this, we can reeducate ourselves to use the emotional rehearsal technique.

To enjoy our business life, we must break out of these conditioned response patterns that are not useful to us and learn new, more appropriate patterns that will contribute to our growth as human beings as well as businesswomen. We have seen that our emotional responses are habit patterns based on beliefs about situations. That's obvious in the example of the blind person who bumps into us on the street. When we begin to experience negative emotional reactions to business situations, we must learn to distinguish between our emotions that are provoked by the situation and the situation itself.

Many of us, for example, react angrily and defensively— perhaps even with tears—when we are criticized for the way we handled a specific project. These emotional responses unquestionably retard our careers simply because they reinforce the male stereotype that women are too emotional for business responsibility. Let's look very carefully at the situation in which some aspect of our performance is criticized to see what went wrong.

Everyone in business, man or woman, makes mistakes. Men, in fact, often take pride in their mistakes because they are an inevitable consequence of risk and because the willingness to take risks is essential to success. Ambitious and aggressive men, therefore, are guided by the axiom: "Show me someone who has never made a mistake and I'll show you someone who has never taken a chance." Men take risks and endure mistakes in order to enjoy successes, and those who are successful accept criticism of their errors with equanimity, knowing that it is a specific decision that is under fire and not their competence as business executives.

Not so with most women. We often react emotionally and defensively to criticism because society hasn't offered us what it has offered to men—the opportunity to develop confidence in our own self-worth. We become defensive when criticized because our whole social psyche has led us to become defensive. To women, it is typical that criticism of a specific action or error is an attack on our worth and competence as human beings. Many of us are desperately fearful of risk, as evidenced by the stereotype of the executive women who adhere strictly to company policies from which men will deviate at the drop of a hat if it is necessary in order to achieve success.

For example, when a woman in sales is told by her supervisor that she handled a specific customer badly, she usually does not perceive this as an effort to help her improve her future performance and thus her career potential. Instead, she tends to react as if her value as a human has been called into question. That, of course, is not the situation at all. Her boss was simply pointing out that one fragment of her total performance could stand improvement and even if his criticism was not constructive it is important not to escalate it. He was not passing judgment on her total value as an employee. Because her belief about the situation was faulty, she might react in an inappropriate and personally damaging way.

Let's look now at a specific technique of emotional reeducation to deal with situations of this sort. The first step is to teach yourself to see situations rationally and to get in touch with the belief systems that are causing inappropriate emotional reactions to surface.

Assume that your boss has been critical of some aspect of your performance and you have reacted defensively because you believe that it is your overall competence, rather than a single action, that has been challenged. Sit down at your desk with a pad and pencil and write a brief but accurate summary of exactly what was said. Record the event as though it were being filmed by a movie camera, without injecting any subjective attitudes or beliefs. It must be a purely objective report of the incident as it occurred.

Next, write your beliefs and attitudes about the event: what you believe your boss's intentions were and what it told you about his attitude toward you.

Third, describe in writing your emotional response to the situation and the feelings you experienced during the episode.

Fourth, ask yourself if your emotional response was one you want to exhibit again if a similar situation occurs in the future.

Finally, write down what you think an appropriate emotional or, better still, unemotional response would be.

Getting all these details on paper will help you to stand outside yourself and look objectively at the event and the reactions it produced. Reviewing this example, the objective facts probably were that your boss said he was not pleased with a project you submitted. In response, you most likely concluded that he was saying you were dumb or incompetent or ineffective; that he was out to punish you, or that he didn't believe that women should be in business, or any one of a number of other reactions based on your own life experience.

You probably reacted defensively because you read into the situation a whole range of issues that maybe weren't there, making yourself miserable and confirming any prejudices your boss may already have had about the instability of women. This was neither a desirable response, nor one you want to repeat, because it could only have an adverse impact on your future prospects in the job. A more appropriate response, in terms of your future career interests, would have been to ask what his specific objections were. If you then chose to justify your reasons for doing it the way you did, it would have been important not to be overly defensive about it. You would tell him that you appreciated his suggestions and thank him for the time he spent explaining his views. If you had worked hard on the project and thought you had done it well, this sounds almost impossible to do. *Yet men do it.* They know that to get angry and defensive with a superior is not smart if they want to get ahead.

Your problem will be to put this perception to work when another similar episode occurs. Knowing how you should respond and wanting to respond that way are useful attributes, but your instinctive emotional response patterns have a firm hold on you and it will be difficult to change your behavior simply because you know what the appropriate emotional response should be.

This phenomenon of knowing how you want to react and finding it virtually impossible to act that way is what the psychologists call cognitive dissonance. You know what you should do and promptly do the opposite. The solution to your problem is a technique called *emotional image rehearsal*. Simply stated, it's a specific mental exercise to rid yourself of a habit or to learn a new one. Research has shown that this is one of the quickest ways to learn or change an emotional response. If you practice emotional image rehearsal daily, you'll learn ten to twenty times as fast as you otherwise would and with about one-tenth the normal effort. Emotional image rehearsal is a shortcut that speeds you through your period of cognitive dissonance by providing the mental map you need to learn a new habit pattern and to do it as quickly as possible.

Emotional Image Rehearsal Technique

The relaxation technique you learned earlier is an important prelude to your experience with the emotional image rehearsal technique. Get comfortable, go through the relaxation technique, and when you are calm, picture in your mind the earlier conflict situation in which you were unhappy with your emotional response. Replay the whole episode in your mind in detail, but exhibit the behavior you desire and actually feel as you want to feel in the situation.

During your image rehearsal, it is very important to actually feel the emotion you consider appropriate in this situation. Repeat this process over and over, while in a relaxed state, for ten minutes at a time. If you feel yourself beginning to get upset as you relive the episode, stop the process immediately and go through the relaxation technique again. When you are relaxed, return to the emotional image rehearsal.

Don't get discouraged, because emotional reeducation does not happen overnight. You have years of reinforced behavior to work with. Most people give up in the cognitive dissonance state—doing what is rationally right but feeling as if it's wrong. It's like learning to drive on the opposite side of the road in a foreign country. It's right but feels awful for a while until you get used to it. It will take some time and a lot of repetition but if you plod onward with this technique it can have a tremendously positive effect, not only on your work life but your personal life as well.

The use of this technique is not limited to the reeducation of emotional responses that you have already experienced. You can also use it to practice appropriate responses to tense situations that have not yet come about. For example, you can use it to prepare yourself for an employment interview. Role play the whole interview in your mind, practicing the response you will make to the questions that are almost certain to be asked.

The use of this technique will greatly increase your chances of feeling and responding exactly as you wish to in most real-life situations, but it will not work unless you practice it. I've found that I can develop the technique while riding the train to work, while stuck in a traffic jam, during a bath, or at any other time when I have a few minutes to relax.

The Persistent Patty Technique for Difficult Situations

We know that to get ahead in business we must break out of the traditional female mold. One element of that stereotype is that we are passive and docile creatures. By becoming assertive, we not only detach ourselves from the stereotype but also take positive action to achieve our goals.

Because we have not been programmed through our lives to be assertive, many of us have difficulty in handling conflict effectively. We are apt to sit by and passively surrender our ideas and beliefs when they meet with forceful opposition, and to put up with unreasonable demands made by others. We get bogged down in explanations of what we want and why we want it. Some of us even experience feelings of guilt about resisting the opposition of those who try to keep us from doing what we want to do.

An excellent cure for this unrewarding trait of passivity is mastery of the Persistent Patty technique. You get what you want by talking like a broken record, persistently sticking to your point, and repeating it over and over.

Persistent Patty ignores all of the side issues and persuasive logic of her opponent and calmly and quietly repeats her argument or demand over and over. Throughout she is totally calm and speaks without a trace of emotion. Consider her technique in a situation in which you need a business report from a male peer who may not want to deliver it in time to meet your requirements. The dialogue may go something like this:

You: John, I need that report you put together covering our most recent sales figures. I must have it by three o'clock this afternoon so I can include it in my presentation.

John: I'm sorry, Sara, I won't be able to give it to you by then because I have to check over the figures again and I'm really tied up today.

You: I can see, John, that you're very busy. But I have to have the report by three o'clock.

John: I told you I don't have time to do it.

You: (Still with great calm) I understand that you told me you're busy, John, but I must have the report by three o'clock.

John: Well, this other work I'm doing is more important and it's for my boss. I don't see how I can do the report for you today.

You: I understand, John, that your other work is important. However, I still need the report by three o'clock.

This a typical instance of the Persistent Patty technique. On the surface it may seem ridiculous, but those who use it almost always get what they want and there are no emotional outbursts. You remain calm while you quietly drive your opponent up the wall. If your opponent becomes emotional, continue to maintain your composure. This reversal of the stereotyped roles will get him in trouble because when anyone becomes emotional in a situation demanding reason, he or she is at a disadvantage. In the end, you'll probably get the report because he can find no other acceptable way out of the situation.

You can learn this technique easily by practicing it with a

friend. Once mastered, it can be used to get what you want in personal as well as business situations. It has the added virtue of helping you earn the respect of your opponents, to say nothing of increasing your respect for yourself, and practicing it can actually be fun. Try it when you have a conflict situation when you're returning merchandise or ordering in a restaurant or grocery store. With practice, you can become very comfortable with it, however inane it may sound, and after it has yielded a few victories you won't hesitate to use it.

One of the most important virtues of the Persistent Patty technique is that it enables you to maintain your self-respect. You will feel good about your firmness, even if you don't achieve your objective immediately. Because it makes you feel good about yourself, your ability to cope with conflict will snowball. Most important, when you have worn down your opponent with the Persistent Patty technique the conflict can be settled on the basis of the real issues rather than on the relative strength of character of the participants involved. That's why it's of such great advantage to a woman who, in most confrontations with men, is perceived as being the weaker personality.

Even if you don't get exactly what you want from this technique, you probably can achieve a workable compromise—and look at what you have gained! You have won at least a partial victory, and you leave the battlefield feeling good about yourself. Women in business cannot always control the results, but we can control our method of fighting for them. The Persistent Patty technique is one way to be assertive, and it often will get us what we want.

The Agreeable Annie Technique

Persistent Patty has a friend named Agreeable Annie who has also proved herself to be a powerful ally. The Agreeable Annie technique is one in which you refuse to be defensive when criticized, refuse to be apologetic, and refrain from counterattacking with criticism of your own. You handle criticism assertively simply by offering no resistance.

This also may sound silly because, at first glance, it seems to be an extremely passive way to handle criticism. What's important is the fact that it works.

Let's suppose that one of your more overbearing male peers challenges you with the comment "Your attitude has been terrible lately." Your normal response to this affront might be an angry, emotion-charged retort like "Well, your attitude would be rotten, too, if you had all the work I do." Having provoked an emotional response, which was precisely his purpose, your adversary now has you at a disadvantage. He'll respond with a further put-down and the dispute will go on, with your responses becoming more emotional with each exchange. Meanwhile, you will have reinforced the conviction of any bystanders that you are the typical woman—emotionally unstable.

Agreeable Annie wouldn't react in this predictable way. She would respond to the same criticism of her attitude with a comment like "Yes, I can see how you might say that." Where does her critic go from there? She has appeared to agree with him without actually doing so. She has not denied his assertion nor has she admitted that he is right. He tried to aggravate her but, in the end, he is the one who is put down. Instead of establishing the basis for a running feud, which she would probably lose, Agreeable Annie has taught her opponent a lesson, earned his grudging—though silent—respect. Probably he will never challenge her again.

The Agreeable Annie technique also works with your boss. Let's suppose he says to you, "You didn't do too well in our two o'clock meeting." An appropriate response might be, "You're right, I wasn't very skillful in the way I handled the situation, was I?" Then, be assertive. Follow up by asking "How do you think I should have handled it?" Because he probably expected a defensive argument, your boss will be completely disarmed. You'll get some valuable suggestions that will be helpful in the future, you'll have won his respect for accepting criticism gracefully, and he'll be pleased and flattered because you sought his advice.

At any job level in the company, it is important that you be able to handle criticism effectively. One of the most prevalent female stereotypes, as we have seen, holds that, when a woman is criticized, she immediately becomes hostile and defensive. The Agreeable Annie technique will separate you from that stereotype by helping you to avoid all of the negative emotions that you otherwise might have displayed when criticized.

The Agreeable Annie technique has other values, as well. It will teach you to hear exactly what your critic says so you can repeat it. You will learn to respond to exactly what is said, not to what may be implied, or what you believe the criticism implies. It teaches you to listen to words, not try to read minds. This eliminates the tendency found in many women of interpreting what is being said to conform to their own self-doubts and insecurities.

The Agreeable Annie strategy is also fun to use. A great way to become proficient at the technique is to role play it with a friend, or if you prefer to practice by yourself, you can use imaginary rehearsal to practice it in your mind. Simply visualize someone criticizing you and respond with your Agreeable Annie technique. It may seem incredible, but when you become a proficient Agreeable Annie, the discomfort of those on the receiving end and your own feeling of confidence and self-esteem will be so rewarding that you'll actually begin to enjoy being criticized. Try the technique and you'll see.

The Agreeable Annie technique will also teach you to accept responsibility for errors without feeling demeaned by the experience. It is essential in business to recognize that you are human and that part of being human is to make mistakes. As noted earlier, one of the stereotypes of women in business is that we are afraid to take risks to achieve important goals. As women, we need to learn to take the necessary risks and then be assertive in coping with our mistakes when they occur. We need to be wary of nonassertive peers who try to manipulate our feelings of guilt and anxiety about making mistakes. In their own insecurity, they often try to reduce more assertive peers to their own level. Don't let them exploit your normal fears by forcing you to seek forgiveness, deny the mistake, or throw out some countercriticism that provides them with a punching bag they can use to work out their own frustrations. Use the Agreeable Annie technique to deal with them.

One very special use of the technique is in cases where we suspect that a male employer may be attempting to manipulate us by using compliments. For example, an otherwise unobservant boss may suddenly say, "Gosh, Annie, you look terrific today. That color is perfect on you." And then, as you succumb to feelings of gratitude for this complimentary attention, he'll add, "By the way, Annie, would you mind working late tonight?"

Because of our early training, it is very difficult for most of us to deny a request from a man who has had the grace to compliment us on something as important as how we look. To say "No" in these circumstances probably would make us feel guilty and anxious. We have an alternative in the Agreeable Annie technique. Instead of refusing the request, we can say, "Yes, I like this dress too, but tell me what it is about it that appeals to you."

If your boss is trying to manipulate you by paying an insincere compliment to achieve a desired result, he will be confounded by this question. He'll be so busy trying to concoct a believable reply that he may even forget that he asked you to work late that evening. Next time you feel that someone is trying to manipulate you by using insincere flattery and you feel like having some fun, try this technique. You may have to work late anyway, but at least you'll have let them know that you're not gullible.

The "Don't Make Them Wrong" Technique

One of the dangers in your relationships with others who are important to your career progress is that of confrontations in which positions become so hardened that neither party can gracefully compromise or retreat. One of the first lessons learned by professional negotiators on both sides of the bargaining table is never to force the other side into a position it cannot abandon without losing face. This can arise in many business situations.

For example, if you and your boss disagree about the solution to a problem, two things can happen. You can have a calm, reasonable discussion in which both points of view are explored and a decision reached on the basis of the facts as each of you now understands them, or one of you can challenge the position of the other and assert that it is totally wrong.

In the second of these situations, bear in mind that the facts haven't changed, but the possibility that you will reach a mutually agreeable solution, without rancor, has been materially reduced. This is true because nobody likes to be wrong and many people will simply not admit that they are, particularly to a subordinate. Try, always, to remember not to place any of your peers or superiors in a position where they have to admit that they are wrong in order to adopt your suggestion.

Many studies have noted the incredible extremes to which people will go to defend an indefensible position in order to avoid being proven wrong. Men routinely have trouble with this problem in their relationships with each other, and because of all the nuances involved in the male and female stereotypes in our society, the situation is infinitely more dangerous when a man and a woman are involved.

Remember, although it will not be ever thus, men still hold the power in the business world. We want to get that power behind us not against us, so it is wise to avoid tramping on their egos.

Consider the example of a woman management trainee who is invited to a meeting. When she arrives, her boss asks her to take notes. As a management trainee, she does not feel that this should be part of her job, particularly when three male management trainees are present and none of them was asked to do it.

She is concerned that taking notes may present her with an image problem, reinforcing the stereotype held by most men that women are only competent in supportive roles in business situations. But if she confronts her boss with the fact that she is a management trainee, not a secretary, and that she believes he is wrong in asking her to take notes, she will put herself in a difficult spot. Because she has accused him of being wrong, he will feel he must defend himself, justify his decision, and enforce it. This also may alienate him and affect his future judgment of the trainee.

Using the Don't Make 'Em Wrong technique, the trainee would handle the situation differently. She might say in confidence, after the meeting, "Mr. Jones, I've really got a problem and I need your help. I have no objection to taking notes in meetings because I know they are important. My problem is that, as the first woman management trainee you have hired, it may position me—in the minds of the men who are present—as a clerical type rather than a professional. That won't help me in my relations with them, so I am trying very hard not to get in that role. I don't want to refuse your request, but I'd like your advice on how we might handle the situation."

You are now in a position where you have not forced him to defend himself against you but instead have entrusted him with the responsibility of trying to help you. Moreover, you have helped him recognize a problem that very likely hadn't occurred to him before. If there is any universal characteristic of male businessmen, it is their consuming dislike for unsolved problems. The odds are he'll solve the problem for you—and for himself—by calling in a secretary or turning the job over to one of the male trainees for the next meeting. If he makes the latter choice and a precedent has been established, later you can volunteer to take your turn—not because you are a woman but because you are also a trainee.

The overriding problem-solving motivation of business people is one you should never forget. You are really trying to solve your problem by getting your adversary on your side of the table. This is the situation you want to be in with your boss. If you succeed in that, you can be virtually certain that together your problem will be resolved.

A friend of mine is fond of demonstrating this problem-solving drive of business executives by placing a sheet of paper in front of each place at the conference table in advance of a meeting. On each sheet, he has drawn three straight lines in the shape of the letter "U." Without exception, when they take their seats, each person at the table will draw a fourth line, converting the letter to a nice, neat box. Businesspeople simply can't stand to see work unfinished or a problem unsolved, and that trait can be of great value to you.

You will make progress in your company to the extent that those in power recognize your ability, respect your behavior and attitudes, and support your desire to rise in the ranks. It will take a lot more effort to rate that kind of recognition and support by making waves. The rewards—money, promotions—come when you earn a reputation for solving problems, not creating them, and when the reputation has earned you the support of those around you. Obviously, there will be many occasions when there is legitimate conflict with your peers and superiors and you cannot abandon your position in these situations. The trick is to win gracefully without undermining your relationship with any of those involved.

This is another skill you can develop through role playing or the emotional imagery technique.

All of the techniques I have outlined in this chapter can be valuable tools in your efforts to advance your business career or to make your present job more rewarding. Not only do they provide you with practical skills, but most of them also will help you escape many of the negative stereotypes that most men have regarding women. Use them during your business hours—and don't overlook the fact that most of them will also work in your personal life. They will increase your ability to get along with your husband, friend, lover, or others who are close to you.

7

How to Gain Self-Confidence and Be Recognized

Self-confidence is the trait that separates winners from losers. It will be the crucial factor in your quest for success in business. With it, your potential can be almost unlimited. Without it, your chances of rising above the pack or enlarging your rewards are minimal if, indeed, they exist at all.

More than anything else, self-confidence is the product of your self-image; the perception you have of yourself. If you believe yourself to be truly competent, productive, and worthy, you can develop great self-confidence. If you have self-confidence you will also have the courage to take the risks on which success can be built. If you experience success it will build further self-confidence which, in turn, will breed more successes. From this process will emerge a glorious concentric circle of personal achievement, with momentum and centrifugal force that enlarges your success with each revolution.

"But," you protest, "how do I get started? How can I build my self-confidence when there is so little opportunity in my daily experience to do things that society considers important, or even worthwhile?"

For many women the quality of life, the successes they achieve, and the failures they experience, are a consequence of self-fulfilling prophecy. If they believe they can succeed, they do. If they expect to fail, they will. Life for all of us is like starting the day by getting up on the wrong side of the bed. If one is convinced that the day is going to be bad it will be, whatever happens, because each of the day's events and experiences will be interpreted from a negative point of view.

Many women greet their business experience as they would a day on which they got up on the wrong side of the bed. We become so preoccupied with the obstacles that lurk in the male business environment that we fail to plan a route around them. The obstacles *are* there, of course, but a women's ability to deal with them depends on having the confidence to do so, rather than the expectation that we can't.

For most women a business career is either a tough row to hoe, or an exciting, challenging one, depending on your point of view. Not only must we deal with the culturally programmed chauvinism of the men around us, but we lack the support mechanisms available to them. Consider the typical male business executive—a comfortably married male. Our culture has been arranged so that he can work all day, served by a clerical support system that is mostly female, and then go home to a second support system, also female. Ideally, when he arrives his martini is waiting to be poured, the food is ready for the table, and his children are poised to feed his ego with their eagerness to see him—but before they can intrude too severely on his evening of relaxation they are rushed off to bed. His most trying hour is the one in the morning that falls between the first cup of coffee brought to him by his secretary at the office, and the last one his wife served him at home.

But what about the married working woman? She has all the business responsibilities her husband has, but too often is without a support system at the office, and still serves as his support system at home. He is free to spend his evenings broadening his intellectual horizons while she tends to the menial chores that wait accusingly around their house. If the marriage falls apart because he thinks his intellectual growth surpasses hers, she is at fault for not keeping up with his progress. If she does keep up with him she must neglect her household duties to do it, and then she experiences negative feedback because her house is less well-kept than those of her nonworking neighbors. Meanwhile, she has feelings of guilt about neglecting her children, and often turns herself into a Super-Mom who tries to do more for her kids than nonworking mothers do. She becomes tired, discouraged, and frustrated, and this, in turn, affects her performance on the job. Ultimately her sense of futility at both home and office leads to expectations of failure and the total destruction of whatever self-confidence she may once have had.

This may seem an exaggerated case, but most of us have experienced some of these emotions, and some working wives have lived through all of them. Small wonder that many of us feel powerless outside our traditional role, or that we lack self-confidence as a result. The first step if you feel you lack self-confidence, or believe you are losing it, is to take stock: try to identify the beliefs you have about yourself that are at the root of the problem. You will probably discover that subconsciously, you have somehow begun to think of yourself as an inadequate person. If so, a good technique is simply to say to yourself, in a very loud voice, "STOP!" Then proceed to identify and evaluate all of your irrational beliefs about yourself that are causing your negative feelings.

Women often hold negative views of themselves because we have the perfection instinct; any performance or behavior that isn't perfect to us is no good at all. We can't perceive failure at a task for what it is—one failure among many successful accomplishments. Instead, we identify our whole being with the single failure, thus losing our self-esteem and consequently, our self-confidence.

If you are to develop self-confidence you must learn to expect that you will do some things well and others badly.

Remember, as you discovered earlier, that men have a great advantage in dealing with self-image. They have been taught early in their lives, through team sports and other activities, that it is all right to lose. "It's not the game but how you play the game that counts," is the creed instilled in them early childhood.

In early adolescence it is the boy who puts his ego on the line to ask a girl on a date. Sometimes she says no. The boy's vanity may suffer a momentary dent, but he has learned to repair it immediately with another call to a girl who says yes. Because boys learn early on to accept failure, rejection, and defeat, they can tolerate all of these experiences without loss of self-confidence when they encounter them in business situations.

Some of us today have an additional role problem for the first time in our lives. The women's movement, with its focus on progress, equality, and achievement for women, has cast a shadow on many female social roles that once were considered quite acceptable to the women who were in them. Many homemakers and women in the lower echelons of business, who once were reasonably content with their lot, have begun to ask themselves—consciously or unconsciously—what they are achieving in their lives. They work as hard or harder than men, but the major rewards—prestige, money, praise, personal freedom—go to men. For women who really want to do more with their lives, and have the capacity and the will to do it, this possibly is a healthy development. For some, the feminist movement has become a two-edged sword, and their sense of self-worth is being cut up by its backswing. They may like what they are doing, but suddenly, they can no longer feel proud of doing it.

It may also be a two-edged sword for those of us who view our self-image as diminished (by feminist depreciation of woman's role in society), causing us to lose self-confidence as a result. Neither of these results is intended by the feminist movement, of course. The women's movement has, in fact, become a powerful ally for those women who want to expand their horizons. But it can be totally demoralizing for those who react to its message with feelings of inadequacy and insecurity, and experience loss of the self-confidence they may once have had.

Because of the opportunities opened up by the women's movement, some women are beginning to feel guilty about the fact that they aren't doing more with their lives. Even women who are already in the working world, perhaps in the typing pool, may find themselves asking, "What's the matter with me? Why am I sitting here in the same old job while other women are moving all the way to chairman of the board?" They don't realize that there is nothing wrong with remaining a typist unless they really want to be something else.

Housewives, meanwhile, may feel that their value to society has been challenged because of the emphasis on nontraditional careers. Once they begin to see their homemaker role in a negative light, they may become even more disturbed by growing concern about how well they are performing it. With the ever-growing divorce rate, and more and more younger women choosing not to marry or have families, they may begin to feel terribly threatened. Tragically, many women feel inadequate and frustrated with their lives despite the fact that they have no desire to get out of the situation they are in. They want to be what they are, but are no longer comfortable with that because they feel they should have higher expectations of themselves.

It is important that every woman recognize that today's values are in transition, that no one knows what tomorrow's values will be. No woman should feel inadequate about her traditional contribution to society simply because options are opening up for women to do other things. New opportunities should be seen as expanding the horizons of women who want to reach out, not as standards of performance against which the past or present performance of others must be measured. You should not feel that, unless you accomplish something more than success in your present role, you are a failure. If you understand that, today's freedoms will permit you to choose the life style that makes you happy and comfortable without loss of self-confidence. What's more, that may well be the role you are already in.

Those of us who genuinely lack self-confidence can do something about it. To begin this process we need to experience our first positive feelings of success. You can develop those feelings by using the emotional image rehearsal process.

If you are not sure you have mastered this technique, go back to Chapter 6 and study it again. You begin, remember, by employing the relaxation technique to unwind and clear your mind of extraneous thoughts and concerns. When you are fully relaxed, try to recall and visualize clearly an incident from the past in which you acted positively and confidently, achieved success with this behavior, and felt rewarded because of it.

This technique works only if you literally relive the incident, not just remember it. The result is a sort of "instant replay" in your mind. Try to recall the most minute details of the experience: Dredge out of your memory the people who were there, how they looked, how you looked, what you were wearing, whether it was day or night, warm or cold, and what your feelings were, moment by moment throughout the experience.

When you have mentally relived the experience itself, direct your thoughts to the feeling of confidence it gave you. Try to experience again the pleasure of succeeding at something and knowing that you had. Become again, in this imagery, the person you were at the time.

Now recall another successful episode. Repeat the process, again reliving the sensation of confidence that your actions and responses gave you. Keep doing this until you have recreated, in one session, a mini-lifetime made up of one successful experience after another. Recognize and analyze the feeling of confidence that it gives you so you can recreate it in subsequent situations.

Now, retaining that confident feeling, move on to step two. Try to imagine a situation that may occur at work in the future, one which you normally might lack the confidence to handle well. Carrying over your feelings of self-confidence to this new situation, imagine it in detail, just as you did the real life situations that had occurred in your past. Create every detail of an office situation as it might happen and deal with it positively and forcefully as you did the situations that you have just relived in your mind. Then experience again the feelings of confidence that pervade your mind. Observe how good you feel about yourself.

Now, mentally aware of the strength and confidence you have the capacity to muster, recreate in your mind a work experience that you handled badly because you lacked confidence in yourself. Imagine yourself in the same situation, but with the self-confidence to handle it differently. Then replay the scene, detail by detail, word by word, but acting your role like the self-confident person you now know you can be. Go through several such incidents, replaying them in detail with yourself in this stronger, more confident role.

You may find yourself, in this third stage, beginning to get uptight and uncomfortable. If so, stop immediately and repeat the relaxation technique. Then relive again a couple of your successes before you return to the situation that troubled you. Your purpose is to erase any negative performance from your mind by replacing it with positive behavior. Then, when you find yourself in difficult business or personal situations in the future, you will be mentally and emotionally prepared to deal with them confidently.

The more you practice this technique the more effective it will be. You must use it until you observe an overall change in the way you feel about yourself in relation to office situations, and observe a change in the way those around you respond to you. Until you do, I suggest you work at it for thirty minutes every day. And don't just plan to do it *sometime;* put aside a specific period each day when you will practice the technique or it probably won't get done.

Once you have developed or restored your feelings of self-confidence, you will probably observe a change in the behavior of the people around you. When you feel good about yourself, those with whom you are associated typically will treat you with more respect, be less manipulative, and communicate with you more directly and honestly. You, meanwhile, will handle conflict situations with greater ease, become more assertive in business discussions, have more influence on your subordinates, peers, and supervisors, and have much more fun.

Remember, self-confidence is synonymous with self-respect. If it is obvious to your associates that you don't respect yourself, it's only natural that they won't respect you, and if they don't respect you it is unlikely that you will be able to influence them or their decisions.

As your feelings of self-confidence increase you can use the emotional image rehearsal technique to place yourself in a whole range of future situations in which it will be important for you to perform effectively. You may want to increase your visibility by giving a speech or making an oral presentation. Practice these activities in your mind, imagining the subject, visualizing the audience, the location, even the faces of those in the front row. Practice running a meeting, or asking for a raise, or bidding for a promotion. In the latter two areas, especially, self-confidence will be the foundation for success in implementing the suggestions that I will offer in the next two chapters.

Once you have a positive belief pattern going for you self-fulfilling prophecy will begin to take effect. You will be confident because you believe you are confident; you will succeed because you know you can succeed. But you must also couple this new feeling of confidence with an outward appearance and behavior that displays you as a confident person. Improve your eye contact with others, cultivate a voice that projects, assume a relaxed posture that does not display you as tense or nervous, offer your hand immediately when you are introduced to someone new, and try to be outgoing in a firm but nonabrasive and relaxed manner. But don't overdo it. You don't want to be too slick—people will get suspicious!

Among the women I have counseled, I have found many who found it difficult to accept my insistence that a psychological technique that seems so simple could really change the course of their lives. I know it can because I have used it myself and have watched it work for countless others.

The first of these was a former roommate named Carol. She held a clerical job in an office in Chicago, but had a burning ambition to get into the fashion world. However, because her self-image was low, she lacked the self-confidence to do anything about it.

One day, by chance, she met someone who could arrange an interview with one of Chicago's major retailers. She was overjoyed by the prospect, which offered an opportunity to get into fashion at a higher level, rather than via the long, tedious route up through a merchandising organization. At the same time, however, she was terrified when she contemplated the interview.

Carol's desire was so strong that she was prepared to accept many of the suggestions that I make in this book. She learned the relaxation technique and the process of emotional image rehearsal. She prepared herself for the interview by taking out stacks of books on fashion merchandising from the library. She reviewed her career and identified a number of experiences which she could use to support her claim that she was qualified for a fashion position. With these resources at hand, she rehearsed her interview with me, developing confidence as she went along.

Although there were a number of experienced competitors, Carol got the job. This further strengthened her self-confidence and she performed so well that she soon was lured away to an even more responsible position in New York. Had she been unwilling to dedicate herself to the task of developing self-confidence, she would probably still be working in the typing pool.

In the clerical role, Carol was typical of many women who have the potential to do more for their company but don't project it to management. Because these women don't appear to have a lot of confidence in their ability in their present jobs they are excluded from consideration for more responsible ones. Most of us were trained to be successful in those areas traditional for women, but lack confidence in our ability to perform well in the skills and attitudes important in business. For example, because society teaches us that it is all right to sit back and wait for direction from others, we are not inclined to be venturesome and assertive. Yet these are qualities that are essential to success in business. How many times have you heard that a man was promoted because he was a "self-starter"? That simply means that he accepts responsibility without being told to do so.

How to Avoid Being "Taken for Granted"

Self-confidence is also an important element in satisfying the need that all of us have for recognition. One of the most common complaints of women in business is, "My boss takes me for granted." They fail to appreciate that there is a clear psychological basis for his attitude. It is a human trait to place a lower value on things we already have, or things we expect to happen.

When you meet someone new you are charmed by his "good traits," and very appreciative of them. But as time wears on, the good traits lose their emotional charge because you have become accustomed to them, and the faults and blemishes begin to appear. When you buy a new car you treat it with great respect until you get used to it, and about that time it begins to get a wash job once a week or once a month instead of every other day.

The same rule applies to your boss. Even if you are a magnificent performer, you need to keep rewinning his appreciation by subtly calling his attention to how valuable you are. You can do this by anticipating his needs in unexpected ways, assuming functions without being asked to do so, or otherwise performing in ways that are productive and helpful, but outside the normal pattern of your relationship with him.

If you feel that you are being taken for granted, and that because of this you will not be perceived as a candidate for a raise or a promotion, you need to take some positive steps to make those at higher levels recognize how valuable you are. For example, you might tell your boss one day, when he is relaxed and not pressed for time, that you are devoted to your career and that you want to meet his expectations in every way. He'll probably nod pleasantly and tell you that he appreciates your devotion.

You now have forced him to think about your relationship and to agree that your performance is important to the company and to him, but don't let it rest there. Tell him that to be certain that you are meeting his expectations you need a complete understanding of what those expectations are. If you are really as good as I'm assuming you to be, this will give him a very bad time. In the process of trying to outline his expectations he will discover the extent to which those expectations are already being met, and he will have a new appreciation of the excellent job you are doing for him.

If he does succeed in identifying areas in which he believes you can be of greater assistance, you obviously will begin to work on them. And as you make progress, you will keep reminding him of the efforts you are making to respond to his expectations. Meanwhile, he will be more aware of the things you were already doing well. You have taken steps to avoid being taken for granted any more.

Know Your Boss's Personal Rules
Every large organization is almost throttled by rules, and the

probability is that your boss has some additional personal rules of his own. Often, he may be unaware of them, but they nevertheless exist.

He may be a stickler about being on time. He may be a "clean desk man," who is appalled when anything on his desk or yours is out of place. He may have preferences or dislikes about personal appearance such as makeup, hairstyles, or attire. His preferences and phobias may extend to countless minute details and although he may not be conscious of them, the cumulative impact of your recognition and response to them will subtly influence the way he feels about you.

You will enhance the prospects that your boss will develop a positive image of you if you actually develop a list of his priorities—his personal rules—and abide by them. Some of them may be idiotic, but who can't tolerate a bit of idiocy if it gets them to where they want to go? Many businessmen do it all the time, but this whole strategy eludes many women in business.

Be Likable

One of the hazards women face—if they are ambitious, determined, and energetic, but lacking in confidence in themselves— is that of taking their work and the world too seriously. It is one thing to present a businesslike appearance and another to become so obsessed with achievement that all of your human qualities disappear. Part of the problem arises from the female stereotype which causes behavior that is acceptable in a man to become unacceptable to a man when it is exhibited by a woman.

A die-hard chauvinist will instinctively see these differences between businessmen and businesswomen: A businessman is aggressive; a businesswoman is pushy. A businessman is good at details; she's picky. A man loses his temper because he's so involved with his job; a woman is bitchy. When he's moody everyone tiptoes past his office so they won't interfere with his efforts to resolve a problem; when she's moody it's because it's that time of the month. He follows through; she doesn't know when to quit. He stands firm; she's uncompromising and narrow-minded. He's a man of the world; she's "been around." He isn't afraid to say what he thinks; she's overbearing. He exercises authority diligently; she's power-mad. He is closemouthed; she is secretive. He has climbed the ladder of success; there's a different mattress on every rung of her ladder. He's a stern taskmaster; she's hard to work for.

Because of this system of interpretation and selective perception, a smart woman in business should always be aware of the impact of her behavior on others. Obviously, a woman perceived to have all of the negative characteristics described in the previous paragraph would not be very well-liked, nor would this perception advance her career.

It is important for women to be assertive in their quest for success, but it is equally important to take stock occasionally of the manner in which our efforts are being perceived. We need to be liked if we are going to influence those on whom our success in business depends.

The easiest way to determine the qualities that will cause you to be liked and those that won't is to make a list of the qualities that make *you* like or dislike others. Once you have done this, compare these qualities as honestly as you can with your own behavior, begin to emphasize those which will cause you to be liked and eliminate the others.

Have a Sense of Humor

If you refer back to the stereotyped description of a businesswoman you will observe that there is little chance anyone would see her as having a sense of humor. In fact, many women in business don't, and it probably stems from the fact that to be funny yourself or to appreciate humor in others, you need to be relaxed. If you don't enjoy your work it's hard to see anything funny in it.

It comes as no surprise to me that one survey of 200 male executives revealed a sense of humor as one trait they commonly failed to find in businesswomen. Because of the obstacles on our road to business achievement, many of us turn into workaholics, and when we get too single-minded about our jobs our sense of humor is apt to get pushed into the background.

All of us need to step back occasionally to ask whether we are taking ourselves and our work too seriously. Often we can relieve the tension by seeing the humor in a difficult situation, and in doing so we become more human—more fun—to the people with whom we share the problem.

If you observe closely the men who have made it to the top you'll find that, almost without exception, they are able to relax and to see the humor in almost any situation. They may be tough, but they are also likable, and, away from their desks, many of them are swinging personalities. They are the ones who rise in the organization while the more intense males, who get uptight about everything, remain static at the lower or middle-management level.

Remember, though, that there is a difference between seeing humor in a difficult situation, and appearing to be scatter-brained. It's a fine line to draw, but one well worth drawing.

Ask for Projects

There is a growing feeling among successful executives who have made it by working hard and long that today's younger employees aren't really interested in their jobs and will do as little as possible to earn what the company pays them. As an ambitious woman this is not the image you want your boss to have of you. Nothing will disabuse him of this feeling more quickly, and make him have a greater appreciation of you, than asking for meaningful projects and greater responsibility. Better still, don't even ask for more work; just do it. Many women have broken out of the clerical ranks by assuming responsibilities that were beyond their job description and presenting their employers with a fait accompli that was not expected of them. They have enlarged and enriched their responsibilities simply by assuming them, and enhanced their prospects for promotion in the process. I have known situations where women who did this created a position for themselves that did not previously exist.

Keep in mind the advice of Gertrude McWilliams, a former General Motors executive who now handles the Chevrolet account for Campbell-Ewald Advertising agency. It contains several gems of truth for women who want to get ahead: "I'm close to fifty and have been an executive long before it was fashionable for women to be welcomed into the executive suite. What it did for me was to realize early that there are no free lunches in life.

The only way I knew was by working as hard as I could, by being sure I was right as I can be, by being fair and giving my people the credit, and by paying attention."

Remember her words the next time the opportunity to give that extra ounce of effort comes along.

Let Your Boss Know You Support Him

There are really two categories of performance that will help you gain recognition from your boss, assuming that he is aware of it. One is how well you do your work for the company; the other is how well you support him in his own quest for progress.

One way or another be sure to make your supervisor aware that one of your objectives is to help make him or her look as good as possible. With some bosses the simplest approach may simply be to tell them this. Others, however, might be embarrassed if you did, so you will have to indicate this kind of support in more subtle ways.

Self-interest being the motivator that it is, many supervisors will appreciate your support for their goals more than they will your performance for the company. Since most promotions are gained, as it were, on the coattails of the boss who measures your performance, it is very important that he or she feel that you are personally loyal.

At the secretarial level this may be something as simple as never saying "He isn't in yet," when your boss receives a call before his arrival in the morning. At a more sophisticated level it may mean keeping him informed about things he may not know that are making the rounds on the office grapevine. It may even be information gleaned from his competitor's secretary that is important to his progress. It may mean anticipating problems, or solving them in his absence. Whatever it is, be supportive, and make certain that he knows that you are.

Be Reliable

When your boss is in a jam, nothing is appreciated more than having people around that can be counted on. This is particularly true if he or she knows that some sacrifice on your part was required to help take care of his emergency. If you are really dedicated to your career, expect to work late at times, or come in early, or work through lunch, if it is necessary to help your boss out of a jam. That's what he did to get where he is, and if you want to get there, you should be prepared to do it too. The greatest appreciation comes when you give more to your job than was expected.

Anticipate Needs and Problems

Despite their countless rules and bureaucratic organization, most businesses are crisis-oriented. Your boss will recognize and appreciate you if you anticipate problems and are prepared to deal with them. Your ability to do this will grow with experience; your willingness to do it may be a decisive factor in how fast you progress in your career.

If you are at the secretarial level, anticipate your boss's needs and remind him or her of obligations. If you know a trip is planned, make certain that the reservations are made and the tickets are ready, without being reminded to do it. Prepare a memorandum containing the schedule, telephone numbers that may be needed, and if appropriate, the names, schedules, and reservations held by those who may be attending the same meeting.

If a big meeting is coming up and you are aware of information, documents, or other materials your boss may need to handle the situation, don't wait to be asked to get them ready. Begin the preparations, and be ready to respond promptly when he finally gets around to considering what will be needed. This is simply another example of going an extra mile to win appreciation.

Be Pleasant

As human beings, we tend to appreciate those who appreciate us. If you want to be appreciated it is important that you let your boss know that you like and appreciate him or her. Be pleasant and positive, even when the demands of your job may seem to be unreasonable. Attempt to understand your boss's moods so that you can accept the difficult ones with equanimity. If you maintain this kind of attitude the odds are that your boss will reciprocate, you will be appreciated, and the third of your life that you spend working will be a lot more fun!

And when that big vacancy occurs, who knows?

8

How to Get a Promotion

Those who succeed in business—men, as well as women—do so because they know where they want to go, have confidence that they can get there, prepare themselves to succeed, identify the behavior that is rewarded in their company, and win the support of those who are in a position to help them grow.

Many of us, although eager to move up in the organization and assume greater responsibility, don't make it because we assume that if we do good work and are loyal to our employer, promotions will automatically come our way. Instead of assertively seeking greater responsibility, we sit at our desks and do what our mothers taught us to do—wait to be asked. Many of us never are.

The road to success in business—however you define success—is exactly that; an upward career path that leads you through a succession of increasingly responsible positions, each of which teaches you something you need to know on the next rung of the ladder. But even if your objectives stop short of the rung at the top, it is a road through a fiercely competitive jungle, and unless you chart your course carefully, you won't go far before you're brought down by one of its hungry tigers.

You have already learned some methods to help you decide on your field of business interest and locate the job you want. Now the same techniques can be used to identify the position that is your ultimate management objective, at least for now, the career path you must follow, and the skills you will need in order to reach it. The suggestions in this chapter are applicable to any woman in business, unless you are content to stay right where you are. In a later chapter, I will discuss more ambitious strategies you can employ if you are totally career-oriented and your career goals reach to the top of the corporate ladder.

A good way to launch your campaign for upward mobility is to use the decision analysis, and other techniques you have learned, to answer several important questions:

How much responsibility do you want to assume? How much of your time and energy are you willing to spend to achieve career progress? What specific jobs in your company do you think you would enjoy doing? Do you have the needed skills and education to aspire to them? What are the intervening job slots through which you must advance to learn what is needed to reach your ultimate goal? Who are the people who will make the decisions that will determine your progress? How can you win their support? Who are your competitors?

The answers to these questions will determine the boundaries of your ambitions and form your master plan for career progress. It is not enough simply to want to be promoted. You must know precisely where you want to go and how you can get there.

Do a Good Job and Be Sure People Know It

If you are promoted it will be based on the agreement of those in power in your company that you deserve it. You can be doing an excellent job, but if no one knows it or only your boss knows it and he doesn't tell anyone, you'll probably remain right where you are. If you are considered a rabble-rouser or are not liked or are ineffective and unproductive or are perceived negatively for any one of a host of other reasons, your chances for promotion are equally dim.

Your prospects for promotion will be enhanced if you project the kind of image that demands recognition. It must convince those who can help you that your performance at a higher level will be superior to that of any other candidate.

Look Like What You Want To Be

The shrewd career woman will try to look like the perfect candidate for the job she wants. The way you act, dress, and wear your hair will contribute to the overall impression you make on others. You want to impress them as a competent, level-headed, unemotional, career-oriented businesswoman. You won't do it if your image fits the stereotype that most men have of us.

I recall a very bright young woman named Sandy who had been Phi Beta Kappa at a very good college. When she got her undergraduate degree, she was unable to find employment in her professional field so she finally accepted a secretarial position. Then she began working on an MBA, hoping that her boss would recognize her career dedication and professional background by placing her in a management trainee position that was open.

Sandy appeared to have everything going for her: Superior college performance, career dedication as evidenced by her work on the MBA, and top-notch performance as a secretary. By every standard but one, she should have been placed in the trainee position but she didn't get it. Her short skirts and exaggerated hairstyle negated all of the credentials on her educational and employment records.

Sandy has finally discovered her problem and is beginning to look more like a businesswoman. The short skirts have given way to tailored suits and dresses and her entire demeanor has changed. She'll make it one of these days.

Tell Your Boss You Want to Get Ahead

Many of us assume that our bosses or other executives know that we want to move upward in the company. Too often, this is not the case. The career-oriented woman must never let herself forget the stereotyped view of her that is held by most of the men with whom she is associated.

Always remember that men are apt to perceive women as having less commitment to careers than is usually the case. Not only have men been taught that women are not business oriented, but that belief has probably been reinforced by the behavior of some women in business who do not, in fact, expect to devote their lives to business careers. Men may also assume that women are ineligible for jobs involving travel or requiring relocation or those in which essentially physical skills are involved.

If you are presently employed in a clerical/secretarial capacity, most men will probably visualize you only in that role. You will be perceived as having the potential to advance within that job category but not for advancement to positions that are nontraditional for women. If you want to move out of secretarial work, you must escape the stereotype and focus the attention of those with the authority to promote you on what your true goals are.

This is a problem that can best be handled by being assertive and very direct. Make it clear to your boss and other executives at every opportunity that you expect to spend your life in a business career, that you are interested in a specific career path, that you are willing to travel and even to relocate (if you are) in order to advance your career.

Don't complain that you aren't getting ahead. Be very precise about where you want to go and ask your boss for advice and help. Once he is convinced that you are seriously interested in remaining with the company and making progress in it, he'll probably begin to give you the help you need.

Escape the Female Stereotype

Because business has always been an extension of maleness in our culture, it is imperative that you disassociate yourself from the stereotyped female behavior. I have already noted repeatedly the elements of that stereotype but they are worth repeating again because you must deal with them if you are going to achieve success. Men see women as emotional, subjective, intuitive, weak, and indecisive. Every one of these perceived traits mitigates against your prospects for advancement because men believe the required business traits to be rational rather than emotional behavior, objectivity rather than subjectivity, analytical rather than intuitive skills, decision not indecision, courage instead of weakness.

We may know that we don't fit the stereotype but that isn't what counts. The very fact that we are women means that a great deal of selective perception occurs. Because men hold an established set of beliefs about us, their minds will reject any evidence contrary to their beliefs and fit it into a consistent and comfortable pattern that conforms to their beliefs.

Your task is to force them to accept a new set of beliefs; if not about women, at least about you.

Know the Rules

We've already identified two kinds of rules—the company's rules and the boss's rules. Observing both sets is important if you want to win a promotion, but beyond these is still another set of rules that determine who makes it in your company. They may not coincide with all of the stated rules when the chips are down.

In most companies, the stated rules governing promotion involve education, experience, other qualifications, length of service, measurable performance on previous jobs, judgment, and leadership qualities, but if you observe carefully, you'll soon discover that many men who win promotions don't seem to fit these stated qualifications.

The qualities that actually do win promotions vary greatly from boss to boss and company to company. Your job is to identify the winning characteristics that influence those with power in *your* organization. The easiest way to do this is to analyze in detail the qualities and actions of those who do get promoted and look for a pattern. You will soon develop real insight into what top management considers to be important in the people it promotes.

I have a friend who says that when he sees someone on an elevator in his office building with a coat and trousers that don't match, he has seen an employee who isn't going anywhere. There are companies in which close observation will reveal that no one in the executive suite wears brown shoes but everyone wears a vest. In some companies, you make it by faithfully having lunch with the right people, including your boss, and always picking up the check. (Your boss can approve your expense account; someone higher up approves his.) In some companies, you make it by always coming to work early; in others by always working late.

I know one woman who enjoyed her work very much and stayed late almost every night. She found that she accomplished a great deal more in the hour or two after everyone else had left the office. She didn't know it but only one other person in the company worked late—its president.

For about a month, when he left his office at night, the company president noticed her lighted office on the other side of the floor. His curiosity to learn who else was working at that hour finally got the better of him and he stopped by to see who it was. He was startled to find a woman.

Because she was the first woman hired into a management job in the company, he was surprised to find that she didn't fit his stereotyped image and expectations of a woman. He asked her what she was doing in the office so late every night, and she told him that she enjoyed her job and found it helpful to spend an extra hour or two in the empty office to prepare for her activities the following day.

This was precisely the strategy the president had pursued to get where he was, so her reply struck a responsive chord. She, in that one instant, had escaped the stereotype and soon— undoubtedly because of the president's influence—was promoted to a much more responsible post.

This woman succeeded because she had unconsciously observed one of the president's most cherished unwritten rules. You can do it too and without relying on luck, if you identify your company's unwritten rules and use them to your advantage.

Be Likable and Personable

A business may appear to be a monolithic system but when you take it apart, you find that it's really a collection of people. Because business decisions are made by people and because it's human nature to reward those you like and enjoy, it is very important that you be liked by the decision makers in your company.

The informal protégé system is an excellent example of this. I have been told by a number of corporate presidents that they were identified within their first years of employment as potential presidents of their organizations. Some companies actually have structured programs of career development for "high-potential" employees who are considered likely candidates for the top management ranks. Usually these selections are made too early in their careers to be based on accurate judgment of the skills and capacity for leadership that they will develop along the way. Consequently, the choice must be made on the basis of how well their appearance and behavior fits the corporate concept of an executive and how well they are liked by the executives who made the selection.

All of us have known exceedingly competent and overworked employees who are stuck on one of the lower rungs of the business ladder. Often, because of their job dedication and intensity, these people are rather dreary by nature; not the kind of relaxed, outgoing personalities that one would choose to invite to a party. Usually they are also unconcerned about appearance, social graces, and office politics. Because their performance goes unrecognized, these men and women often grow angry about being overworked, develop a martyr syndrome, and instead of being merely dreary, they become literally impossible to like. They may keep their jobs, but they have also foreclosed any possibility of ever getting better ones.

I see this happening every day at the secretarial level. Breaking out of the secretarial field into nontraditional areas of responsibility is a difficult task at best, but for the woman who feels oppressed, neglected, unappreciated, and bitter because of it, and who reflects these attitudes in her relationships with others, progress is all but impossible.

Often this happens simply because a woman is overworked and doesn't have the time or energy to be pleasant. By the time she recognizes that her attitude is holding her back, it is too late. She gets her first recognition when she retires and is handed a corsage and, with luck, a gold watch.

A woman in this situation would be well advised to recognize the effect that overwork is having on her personality and frankly tell her boss that she can no longer handle the load. She'll be better off, even if he fires her, because at least she can then go be likable someplace else.

Being likable, however, doesn't mean becoming the office

comedian or the happy idiot who dances on the table at the annual Christmas party. You want to be liked and respected for performing your job responsibilities capably and with good humor. Businesswomen may be liked by the men in power because of what they see in them as women and get nowhere because the men still feel that they have no business talent whatever.

I once worked with a woman named Maria who was adored by every executive in the office. Although she was extremely talented and performed her job to perfection, she was getting nowhere in the company. Maria and I discussed her situation and it became very apparent why she was still in the same job. While everyone loved her, nobody considered her as a business type. She was liked for a bubbling, outgoing personality and because she was a ball of fun to be around. She laughed and joked with the executives and they enjoyed her immensely as a pleasant respite from an otherwise conservative office, but that very disassociation from business pushed her out of their thoughts when promotional opportunities for which she was qualified became available.

Maria and I agreed that she needed to direct her very pleasing personality into appropriate business channels so that she would be regarded both as an enjoyable person and as an effective businesswoman. Soon her personality took on a totally new dimension. Where, in the past, she had laughed and joked about frivolous things, she now used her sense of humor and sparkling personality to emphasize her business knowledge. Within two months, she had begun a steady upward movement in the corporation.

Develop Your Skills

Another factor that will determine the breadth of your horizons within your company is possession of the skills needed to perform the next level of responsibility. But simply having those skills is not, by itself, enough. Those in power must recognize that you have them. Frequently, we have the skills we need but it doesn't help us because no one knows it. If you are in this situation, you need to determine how you can prove that you are ready to be promoted.

It is also important to recognize, contrary to the beliefs of many of us, that working at one job for a long period of time is not recognized as a qualification for promotion. It may, in fact, lead some executives to conclude that you have been considered for promotion in the past and "passed over." Although seniority may be a factor in jobs that are unionized, considerations of competitiveness, skills, and ability are what count toward promotion to positions that are not.

Let's say you are in a secretarial position and want to be promoted to the next higher level. Your first step is to determine the qualifications for the higher-level job. Chances are, if you check with the personnel department, you will find that the job description is just a broadening of your current responsibilities. For example, if you already have shorthand and typing skills, they will be assumed for the next job level; other qualifications will become more important. At the next level, you may be required to work for more supervisors and assume increased responsibilities. These are not really qualifications that you can train for. You can demonstrate your capacity to handle them only by outstanding performance in your present job that is recognized by those in a position to promote you. This probably will mean working a bit harder and doing a bit more than those around you who are also candidates for the promotion or doing your job differently and more efficiently than the others so that you call positive attention to yourself.

One highly regarded quality in business that becomes increasingly important as you move up the ladder is the ability to perform effectively under pressure. As I have noted, business is crisis oriented and the most valuable people are those who respond well to crises. If you demonstrate the ability to keep a cool head when the pressure is on, your boss is more apt to think of you as a promotable employee.

At the very top secretarial levels, for example, one of the most important skills is the ability to handle people effectively and remain poised in difficult situations. Always remember that the image you present in the office is being observed by others besides those you contact directly, including those who will make the promotional decisions that affect you. If you project the image of a competent, assured, and pleasant executive secretary, your chances of success will be greatly improved. If you have any doubts about what that image should be, observe the behavior patterns of the successful secretaries in your office—those who are obviously already "in" with the boss. Chances are that they already possess the traits that the company management deems necessary for success. If not, they wouldn't be there.

If supervision or management is your objective, don't put off identifying the next rung on your career ladder and establishing a timetable for reaching it. As part of this planning process, you need also to identify the skills that you will need at the next level. If you and your boss have discussed your career objectives, he may help you to identify needed areas of personal development and arrange opportunities for you to acquire the skills you need. Then, as you become qualified for the next promotion, be sure to make this achievement known. If, for example, you have taken a business course to prepare you for your next job level, it is important that your boss and anyone else who is concerned be aware of it. Many companies don't have structured methods of tracking the career development of their employees, so your self-improvement activities may not be part of your personnel file. If you have done development work on your own, don't fail to keep everyone who counts advised of it.

Maintain a Positive Attitude

Although there may be aspects of your job that you find disagreeable or characteristics of your boss that you dislike, you won't enhance your image by discussing them around the office. It is best to concentrate on the positive aspects of your job if you want to get ahead.

One of the unwritten rules of the business game says: "Support your boss or don't take his money." I've seen men driven to psychiatrists' couches because of their inability to deal psychologically with their bosses. The psychiatrists heard the complaints that the rules of the game wouldn't permit them to express at the office.

The reasons are obvious. All business people are primarily dependent on their boss for the next promotion. The boss may not have the authority to grant it but a negative assessment from him could probably stop it. Beyond that, if other executives learn that you are bad-mouthing your boss, you probably won't be welcome in their departments. They reason that if you are openly critical of your present boss, why not them?

In my experience, I've observed that many women have yet to learn this lesson. Perhaps because women are used to being competitive with other women, they will be catty without hesitation and, in many cases, they will talk about their bosses in this manner as well.

Sharing your grievances with others may make you feel better but it won't improve your chances for advancement. An important part of your business image is your attitude. If you appear enthusiastic about your work, you gain points, if you are seen as difficult and negative, you lose them. If you are in a truly impossible situation with your immediate supervisor, don't complain to your co-workers, go to the personnel department and determine the approved procedures for handling this kind of situation.

Use Your Sense of Humor

Perhaps because of the pressures we are under, many women in business lose their sense of humor. We take ourselves and our work so seriously that we aren't even pleasant to be around. This can be a real handicap which can hamper our efforts to move upward because the executives we would report to may conclude that our presence would dampen the spirits of others in their group.

You don't want to seem "giddy" to your peers or superiors, but you should try to maintain a sense of humor about your work and be prepared to use it to advantage in tense or difficult situations. If you don't, you'll be falling into another of the patterns of the female stereotype.

Claudia is an example of a woman who once had a sense of humor but has become so intense about her work that she has lost it. She was promoted from an executive secretarial position directly into a supervisory job, an unusual route to take. Under the pressures of learning the new job, she soon began to develop some unbearable qualities, turning into a workaholic who became unable to discuss anything but the pressures of her job. As a result, she has never progressed beyond that first promotion. She probably won't until she learns to take herself less seriously.

A sense of humor is often invaluable to relieve the tension when you are faced with a troublesome confrontation. Gloria Steinem, a well-known feminist who has more than her share of confrontations with men and women, is a master at turning a tense situation into a humorous one by exercising her ready wit. Men may disagree with her, but they rarely dislike her personally once they have been exposed to her relaxed, easygoing, humorous charm.

Learn the Business Style of Communication

Many corporate chief executive officers impose a rule that they will read no communication if it exceeds one page. Brevity is the rule of communications in business, whether it be written or oral. Observe a successful executive and almost invariably you will find that his conversation is concise, specific, and to the point.

One of our handicaps in business is the perception of men that women speak in generalities, don't have the facts, talk too much, and waste time defending our positions with elaborate explanations. To break the stereotype, we must learn to communicate the way men have been taught to do.

The rules are simple. Speak positively, without ambiguity or superfluous detail. Have the facts and quantify everything you can. Be brief and concise. Stop talking as soon as you know your point has been made, no matter how much more you were prepared to say. Executives abhor subordinates who ramble on with tedious explanations that add nothing to the information already conveyed.

Don't Let Your Boss Hold You Back Because You're Too Good

The most valuable asset of any supervisor or manager is the people who work for him. They determine whether he looks good or bad, rises or falls. Consequently, bosses are sometimes understandably reluctant to lose the people who are providing their most effective support.

If you have been performing exceptionally well, are certain

that your boss regards you highly, but aren't getting ahead, consider whether you are not being recommended for promotion because he doesn't want to let you go. If so, don't wait; act, because there is little chance that the situation will get any better.

Your first step might be to have a frank discussion with your boss. Ask him whether he is satisfied with your performance. He'll have to say yes, unless he's prepared to tell you what's wrong with it, and if you're really good, he can't. Then tell him you are concerned because you have worked for him so long without a promotion. Tell him you have decided to discuss the situation with the personnel department, and if you determine that there is no future for you, you intend to go to another company. Tell him also, that before you do that, you are going to go to his supervisor, who must be responsible for your lack of progress, and voice your feelings about an organization that doesn't provide upward mobility for its women employees.

If you follow this course of action, one of two things will happen. You'll get fired, or you will be asked to be patient for a while before consulting either the personnel department or your boss's supervisor. If it's the latter, you'll probably soon get your promotion. Your boss won't risk being seen as a problem by his boss when he knows he's going to lose you anyway.

This strategy can be very effective but here's one more word of advice in case you have to try it: Wait until you have another job to go to in case it doesn't work.

Find a Godfather

A godfather, sometimes called a mentor, is a highly placed male in the organization who will serve as your counselor, tutor, and critic and support you with other members of executive management. He will teach you the informal structure of the business, keep you supplied with critical information, and help you plan your career strategy.

You may wonder why anyone would assume such a role in your behalf. I believe there are three reasons: First, anything he does that helps you succeed gives him the feeling that he has enlarged his own achievements; second, his reaction to your successes is not unlike that of the proud father whose son makes the Dean's list in college; and third, he is clever enough to know that if he wins your loyalty by helping you now, the time may come as you move up the ladder when you will be able to return the favor by helping him.

Almost every successful male executive has had a mentor during his career. It is even more important for a woman to have one, because she does not have access to many of the sources of information available to competing males. Try to become part of this informal protégé system by identifying an influential male executive who will take an interest in your career. If you get along well with your boss, he may be the one.

Go On As Many Interviews As Possible

From time to time, promotional opportunities may be posted in your company or you may hear of openings that exist in others. Your development will be strengthened if you interview for as many of these jobs as possible, particularly those outside your organization. Each interview adds to your skills in handling this work situation but, more than that, the interviews will tell you something about the expectations employers have of candidates for various kinds of jobs, and the skills you should develop or acquire in order to qualify.

One word of caution: There is some danger in requesting interviews for every opening in your company that comes along, regardless of your degree of interest in the job. If you are interviewed for a long succession of jobs for which you are clearly unqualified and for which you are not hired, management may begin to perceive you as a person who is constantly rejected for promotions because you aren't qualified for anything.

Ask for a Performance Review

If you have gone more than a year without a raise, a promotion, or any indication of how your boss feels about your performance, it is important that you take the bull by the horns and ask for a performance review. Many supervisors are timid about telling employees what their weaknesses are and suffer in silence, muttering to themselves because you do not meet their expectations and silently punishing you by withholding promotions. Obviously, you can't satisfy their expectations if you don't know what they are, and a request for a performance review may give your boss the courage to speak out. It will also reinforce his perception of you as someone genuinely concerned about progress in her career.

Watch for Other Positions

Even though you are satisfied with your present job and company, it is always wise to be alert to opportunities to improve your situation. If your company has a job-posting system, follow the announcements faithfully, because you may discover one that offers the opportunity to make a quantum leap in your career progress.

Watch the positions that are advertised in your Sunday paper for challenging opportunities. This will serve the added purpose of keeping you abreast of the existing supply of people in your speciality and the going compensation rates. Keep your resume current so that you will always be prepared to supply one quickly in response to one of these ads.

No matter how happy you are in your current position, it is shortsighted not to be aware of other jobs and not to place yourself in situations where you may become aware of them. I can give you an excellent example of this from my own experience. At one stage in my career, I had a job in personnel and was sent to a seminar on personnel administration to sharpen my interviewing skills. There were about seventy-five men in the seminar and one woman—me. It was soon obvious that the men assumed that I was there taking notes for my boss, rather than as a full-fledged member of the seminar.

I decided it was necessary to let them know this wasn't true and, to do it, I challenged one of the speakers on a point with which I strongly disagreed. We had a light but lively debate, and my decision to engage in it proved to be one of the wisest I had ever made. Later that day, after lunch, I felt a tap on the shoulder. I turned around and there was the speaker with whom I had debated that morning.

"I think my company can use you," he said. "Would you be willing to come over and talk to us?" I almost declined, feeling that it would be inappropriate to accept an opportunity generated by a meeting my company was paying me to attend. Then it occurred to me that this was typical female logic at work and that no man in my company would react that way.

To make a long story short, I went on the interview and was offered a position to train in an entirely new field that was extremely attractive to me. It would give me an excellent opportunity to broaden my experience and double my salary in the process. Needless to say, I accepted the position.

If I had not been exposed to the opportunity to debate the speaker and if I had not been assertive enough to decide to do so, I would have missed an opportunity to accelerate the development of my career.

9

How To Get a Raise

Your boss is not a fairy godfather who will one day touch you with a magic wand and turn your miserly paycheck into a pot of gold. If you do good work and have the kind of boss who is sensitive to his employees' needs, you may get your raises promptly when you deserve them, but if you work for the miserly type, who makes points by holding costs down at the expense of his subordinates, you may have a problem.

Most of the larger, more structured corporations provide annual salary increases for their employees that recognize seniority and the effects of inflation, and additional increases for selected employees based on performance. Typically, a firm will allocate an annual sum of money based on a percentage of the total payroll for use in recognizing superior individual performance. Individual managers may then allocate this money among the employees in their group as they see fit. If, for example, six percent of payroll is allocated for performance raises, one employee in a group might be awarded a twelve percent raise and another employee nothing. The manager might also decide that the performance in his group was such that he will not use all of the money allocated to him, but that rarely happens because it reflects on his own performance as a manager to admit that his group is not performing well.

At any rate, if you are passed over for a raise, it makes no sense to accept the situation passively and say nothing about it. You may have been passed over because of some negative aspect of your behavior or performance, in which case, you need to know what it is so that you can overcome the deficiencies that denied you the raise. Or, although your performance is good, the boss may have allocated the available money among a group of favorites or he may simply have greased the wheels that squeaked and given performance increases to the employees who were assertive enough to ask for them.

The situation calls for a relaxed confrontation, in which you simply tell your boss that you are concerned because you have not received a raise. Tell him you want to know whether it was because he is dissatisfied with some aspect of your performance so that you can improve it in order to earn more money. It may be wise to use the image rehearsal technique and role play in advance of this confrontation so that you will be relaxed and prepared to deal with any response you may get.

Don't forget, though, that your objective is to get a raise, not to point out that your boss is a jerk for not giving you one. Remember the "don't make 'em wrong" technique when you have this discussion.

Timing

Give some serious thought to the question of when you should ask for a raise. First of all, you should be prepared and relaxed yourself.

Second, you should pick a time when your boss appears to be cheerful and relaxed; perhaps when he has just received a raise himself. Third, try to select a time when the company's profit situation looks good, possibly right after an unusually good quarterly earnings report. Fourth, don't simply make a casual comment to him about a raise or he may just pass it off without taking you seriously. Make a formal request so that he knows you are serious about it and has to deal with the situation.

The Basis for a Raise

Your hand will be much stronger if you ask for a raise at a time when you have recently demonstrated exceptionally capable performance or have been asked to do an unusual amount of work. It is generally a negative approach to ask for a raise simply because "it's been a year since I got the last one" or "I deserve a raise" or "Mary Ellen down the hall just got one."

One strategy that I have found to be effective is to make a list, over an extended period, of all your areas of responsibility, the specific duties you perform, and how you allocate your time. Try to establish that, since your present salary was established, you have taken on additional responsibilities and performed them well and have become a more valuable and well-trained employee of the company. It is a fairly good general rule that the more important you can make your job appear, the greater the compensation management will feel it deserves.

If you have made specific contributions that have enabled the company to perform better, save money, or increase productivity and profit, cite these when you talk to your boss. Try, if possible, to quantify the results you obtained, because most businessmen don't speak English, they speak arithmetic.

How to Approach Your Boss

The actual approach you use in introducing the subject of money will depend on how close a relationship you have with your boss. If it is fairly close, you may want to be somewhat more casual than if it is not. The important thing is to help him see your point, not make him wrong, and have him feel that you have a mutual problem that you must work out together.

You might say, for example, "Mr. Jones, I have a problem I would like to talk to you about. I need to make more money to carry out my responsibilities and I think my performance has been such that I deserve it. You may not agree but, if so, it would help me to know the reasons so that I can improve any part of my performance that is holding me back financially."

You have now registered your need, but without complaining about it or making him wrong, and you have asked for his help. He has nothing to be angry about and can hardly refuse to respond to your request for help. If he has legitimate reasons for denying your raise, you'll probably learn what they are; if he doesn't, he may simply say that it slipped his mind and give you the raise.

If he gives you reasons you do not consider legitimate, you may find the Agreeable Annie technique effective. When he has listed his grievances, respond by saying that you can understand how he might believe these things but that you may have been negligent in giving him enough information about what you are really doing. Then proceed to describe your performance in the best possible light. Make it clear that you are not against him but with him in a joint effort to have both of you look good. You want to create a situation in which you are not adversaries but two people trying to solve the same problem.

For some women, particularly those whose need for additional income is particularly acute, this can be a very trying emotional situation. Sometimes, if the situation becomes too unbearably tense, they actually do break down and cry. If you reach the point where you are about to do that and need to in order to relieve the tension, go ahead but get to the ladies room first, where your boss and your male peers won't see you. Crying makes men uncomfortable and no one likes to be uncomfortable, so, if you do it publicly, it may damage your career.

Other Ways to Make More Money

If money is your primary work objective and you are willing to do almost any kind of work to increase your income, explore your options thoroughly. There are two categories of employment that pay very well; those that require a great deal of education, training, or specialized skills and those that most people don't want to do. In the latter case, compensation is simply following the law of supply and demand: If work needs doing and there aren't enough people to do it, the compensation increases in order to lure more people into this kind of work.

Watch the ads and observe the types of skilled employment that are commanding the highest hourly rate. Remember, ditchdiggers make more than schoolteachers these days. When you have identified the better-paid jobs, study the qualifications needed to obtain them and the ways in which these qualifications can be obtained. You may find that you can take some specialized training that will enable you to enter a new and more profitable field, without having to give up your present job and salary while you are learning. There are some new fields, such as information services, that may offer this kind of opportunity for you. Increasingly, work that used to be done by people is being performed by computers but this has also generated a huge demand for specialized people who can keep the computers humming.

Commission sales, which I have already discussed, is another promising area for those whose primary interest is money. Here, your income is limited only by your own ability as a salesperson, your willingness to work, and making certain that what you are selling is a good and desired product or service.

If you are a career-oriented person, but one who is also concerned about maximizing her income as well as her responsibility and authority, you may wish to get some further education, to change fields, or even to change companies. If so, read carefully the tips for career women that you'll find later in the book.

How to Get the Best Salary Offer

Although most large companies have a salary administration program which defines the compensation considered appropriate for every type and level of employment, there are very few in which the salary ranges for each job are not flexible enough to permit a manager to pay more than average for a highly qualified woman that he really wants to hire. To get maximum compensation, you must, first of all, sell yourself thoroughly and then exercise your very best negotiating skills. Unfortunately, this is not a skill that most of us are very good at because of the passivity training program that society has put us through.

This is really paradoxical because women typically are known to have innate qualities that should make them more skillful negotiators than men. One of these is our intuitive sense, which research is finally revealing as one that is more highly developed in women. Try to use your intuition to determine how badly your prospective employer wants you and how far you can push him in salary negotiations.

You need more than intuition alone. You should try to determine the salary range for the job you are being offered. You may try to convey the impression that you are considering other offers, and that your starting salary is one of the things that will tip the scales as to which you accept. Remember also that there is an Equal Pay Act which requires that you be compensated at a level equal to that of any man employed in a similar job.

Finally, consider very carefully what your response will be if your prospective employer asks you what your present compensation is. If your intuition and other signs tell you that he is really eager to hire you, you may wish to duck this question as best you can to avoid receiving a salary based on your present income rather than what you are worth in a new job to the company that wants to hire you.

If, on the other hand, you are not certain that he is that eager and believe that the level of salary required may determine whether he is willing to hire you, you may have to tell him what you are making in your present job. If so, make sure you include every aspect of compensation such as employee benefits. Also consider telling him not what you now make but what you expect to be making when your next promotional increase comes along.

It is important to get the highest entry salary you can because your employer has considerable flexibility in fixing the level of salary at which you begin. He has very little flexibility with respect to salary increases once you are on the payroll, because these must fit the overall compensation plan of the company. If they are excessive, they cause all kinds of unpleasant emotional reactions among other employees in your category who did not fare so well. For this reason, someone already on the payroll rarely gets a raise so high that it is out of line with what is being given to others in the same category.

As they say, a bird in the hand . . .

10

How to Handle Difficult Situations

The art of management is largely a matter of knowing how to arrive at sound decisions, many of which grow out of difficult situations the individual manager or the company must resolve. Men in business, over time, have perfected certain strategies to deal with difficult situations they or their predecessors have experienced in the past.

Women in business have a different problem because often there is no precedent for dealing with difficult situations. Moreover, because some of them involve our relationships with more powerful men in the organization, solutions are required that will solve the problem without alienating the male decision-maker, who may have the power to aid or block our monetary rewards or our upward progress.

The first rule to follow in handling a difficult situation involving another person is to try to see the problem from that person's point of view. This does not mean that you should agree with the opposition, but simply that you should try to understand where that person is coming from before you try to devise a solution. Otherwise, you may develop a solution to the problem as you perceive it, but not to the one that's really there. Sometimes, when you fully understand the position of the other person you may even discover that the problem isn't there at all. But let's look at some situations that have troubled women in business. Most of these are unique to us.

Going for Coffee

The requirement that secretaries get coffee for their bosses is probably the most publicized problem at the moment. I have seen a range of positions advocated by women's groups that includes telling the boss to go to hell or that it's not in your job description. You could say either of these things, of course, or you might even want to find another secretarial job. But chances are that another job wouldn't help because the odds are that the first request of your new boss would be, "Please get me some coffee."

My assumption is that secretaries who object to getting the coffee feel that their bosses are trying to make gophers of them. Sometimes this may be the case, but I doubt that it is very often. Let's turn things around for a moment and look at the question from the boss's point of view. Getting the coffee obviously isn't the most productive part of the company responsibilities you and your boss share, and it makes sense that it be performed by the one whose time has the lowest monetary value.

Also, recognize that males in business do all kinds of leg work for their bosses, up to and including getting their coffee at times. They don't feel demeaned by that because they recognize the relative value of their time and his, and because they know that their willingness to do what needs doing will be an important element in their boss's perception of them.

If you don't like performing personal services for others, you should take a careful look before you decide to be a secretary. Many bosses expect this service as part of the secretarial contract, and if it bothers you, you may be in a difficult position. To alienate your boss by refusing to do it won't help your future career. But always remember, when you get to be boss you can hire a male secretary to get it for you! There are a lot of problems in business that women have to contend with, so let's channel our energy toward the important ones.

Taking Notes In Meetings

I've already discussed one way of dealing with this one, but I want to add one positive thought that may provide an alternative for you. The spoken words that are exchanged in meetings have value, of course, but it is the concise written record of what transpired that often determines the action that will be taken. Preparing the minutes of a meeting can be the most important single contribution of anyone in the room. If you do it skillfully, you will get credit for it because it is the one element of the meeting that everyone present will review. Moreover, it will give you access to the leader of the group when you review your notes with him and, consequently, an opportunity to impress him with some of your other qualities.

You can choose the other route of not taking notes, but before you do, consider whether you want to sacrifice what could be a golden opportunity.

Typing Your Own Letters

Many women who are hired into management complain that while their male peers have an office and a secretary, they have only an office and a typewriter. The assumption is that because we are women we know how to type, so the company saves a secretarial salary when we do our own typing.

Even though many men, particularly in fields such as public relations, prefer to do their own typing, it is important for women in management to object to doing it. This is obviously a case of escaping the stereotype that we belong in supportive roles, and it's necessary to resist any treatment that reinforces that stereotype.

The time to handle this problem is the moment the typewriter is brought in, not after you've stewed about it for a week or two. Go to your boss and tell him that if the company had been looking for a typist when they hired you they wouldn't have given you the job, because your typing is lousy. Tell him that you think it would be a waste of your higher-priced time to do something badly that a lower-paid secretary could do better.

Finally, tell him that because the company has so few women in management you have a real problem in convincing others that you really have management responsibility. Tell him that you won't be really effective until you have been accepted into the management role, and that doing your own typing will make it more difficult for you to reach that point. Tell him you are sure he will see that the company's interests, as well as yours, will be better served if you share the privileges of your male peers and obviously have equal status with them.

If you put the problem on this basis, rather than engaging in a direct and angry confrontation in which you make him wrong, the odds are that you will get your secretary.

If you handle it the wrong way you may find yourself in the position of my friend Susan, who was employed in the advertising department of a large corporation where a number of the management people did their own typing. When a typewriter was brought to her office she was incensed because she felt her status in management was being demeaned. She made so much noise that they removed the typewriter.

Susan congratulated herself on winning a significant victory until she started trying to get her work done. It wasn't easy, because so many of those on the staff did their own typing that there were very few secretaries. By the time one of Susan's projects had gone through two or three drafts, it had taken her a day or two to do something that one of her peers could finish in a couple of hours.

This, of course, made Susan look bad, so she spent an increasing amount of time hassling the secretaries. They responded to that in predictable fashion, and Susan looked even worse. In the end the department head became so upset with Susan's attitude and her slow performance that she was asked to leave the company.

Sexual Harassment

Almost every working woman I know has been propositioned by one or more of the men in her company. Obviously, there are some situations that can be easily handled. Others can mean real trouble—persistent approaches made to you that are clearly dangerous or that involve men in positions of authority who use their power as a threat.

In most cases you can handle the problem very simply by

saying that you're not interested, and that's the end of it. But if the other person is superior to you in the company, and if he is persistent, you have a problem. Some women solve it by relenting and regretting it later. When this kind of relationship turns sour, proximity becomes intolerable and someone has to leave the company. And it's rarely the man.

How, then, do you deal with a persistently aggressive superior whose support you may need to achieve your own goals? First, you don't reject him in ways that will threaten his ego. If you do you'll certainly alienate him so totally that he will move heaven and earth to make sure that you fail. A more sensible course is to tell him that you are not interested and to give him a legitimate reason so that both his ego and your self-respect remain intact, and he is still your friend and not your enemy.

I have known some instances in which this was not enough. If so, and if his overtures become true harassment, you may have no alternative but to subtly suggest that you are going to report his behavior to his boss. This may end it, but it also will destroy the possibility that your career objectives will get any positive support from him. Another option, depending on your situation, might be to go to the personnel department and try to arrange a transfer to another jurisdiction.

To show that times are changing, I might note that men are beginning to have this problem, too. As increasing numbers of women move into management, there are reports of female bosses who are becoming very assertive and demanding personal involvement with the males who work for them.

Sexual harassment is illegal, and a woman—or a man, for that matter—can file a charge with the government when it occurs.

Male Avoidance

Too little, rather than too much attention from men is a more common problem for most businesswomen. Business is a team effort, and much of its work is accomplished through informal structures—over lunch, on the golf course, etc. It is in these informal situations that much of the most significant business communication takes place. Many a decision is made over a two-martini lunch.

Because business, at the higher levels, has for so long been a male province most of these informal groups are exclusively male. Many of them involve long-standing relationships with peers. It is difficult for a new male employee to break into them, and almost impossible for a woman. She has the greater problem because the men are uncomfortable over her presence, which they feel will restrain their free wheeling, sometimes vulgar conversation.

Yet if a woman in management is excluded from these groups, she is denied an important element of business progress. Excluded from an important communications network, she is unable to participate in a part of the company's decision-making process.

Your best bet, if you have this problem, is to identify the most influential man in the group you want to join and attempt to get his attention and confidence. Ultimately, he can become the advocate who gains your admission to his group. Because he brought you in, you probably will be accepted more readily, and once the others become accustomed to your presence your problem will be over.

This is sort of like finding a godfather who will represent you to top management. It is easier to find one member of a group who will be an advocate for you than to try to influence all the members.

It helps, once you are admitted, to have some common non-business interests and knowledge that will enable you to join in the conversation. One very sharp female executive made this transition into the informal group much easier by faithfully reading the sports pages. She says that the first time she dropped a baseball score on the group the shock registered was enormous. However, when the men recovered they were really pleased that they had something mutual besides business to talk about, and she felt that from then on she was "okay" in their eyes.

Your Boss Dislikes You

If your boss clearly dislikes you and you can't change his mind, one possible solution is to try to get transferred. You need the support of your boss to get a raise or a promotion, and if you quit your job any potential employer will probably call him for a recommendation. Your best bet is to get relocated within the company so that you will have the support of the man you work for in any of these situations.

If your position is such that a transfer is impossible, the only alternatives are to make the best of it or to look for another job. Psychiatrists' couches are continually filled by males who can't stand their bosses yet have to work with them. Perhaps you could get your boss promoted out of your way.

They Won't Let You Buy Lunch

Many working women are disturbed when their male associates won't let them pick up the tab for a business lunch. This is one case where it's imperative that you put yourself in the men's shoes.

Men have been trained from youth to pick up the check. It shatters their ego to be observed by other men allowing a woman companion to pick up the check or even paying for her own lunch. If you break into a male group with whom you lunch regularly, keep volunteering to pay your way but don't embarrass them by being too insistent. If you do they may simply begin to exclude you from the group because you have become a problem to them. If you bide your time and keep offering to pay, the economics of the situation will, after a while, probably cause them to let you spend your money.

This is another area that, to me, seems relatively inconsequential. I'd rather lose a few battles to win the war; in this case, with a little patience, you sooner or later will probably win both.

Business Travel with Men

The thought of having to send women on business trips with male associates is one of the barriers, in many companies, that keep women out of management. It is based in part on the protective instinct that most men have toward women, and in part on fear of the reaction that the wives of male employees will have to women traveling with their husbands.

There isn't much you can do about it except be completely

businesslike about your trips, in the office and on the road. After you have made a few successful trips, the problem will disappear.

You should remember, though, that there is much in the traditional attitude of men toward women that may make your male associate uncomfortable when he travels with you for the first time. Should he sit next to you? Stay at the same hotel? Carry your luggage or attaché case? Give you the inside seat or the outside seat? Take you to a movie if you have a free evening? Recognize these concerns and put him at ease to the degree that you can.

Jokes That Stop the Meeting

A common experience of management women is walking into an all-male meeting in the midst of a gale of laughter and having it change to stony silence the moment you enter the door. In a moment or two someone probably says, "Well, here comes Sally, so I guess we'll have to cut out the dirty jokes." Everyone laughs again, nervously, and the meeting proceeds.

It is an uncomfortable feeling because the implication is that your presence is interfering with the normal conduct of the meeting. Your best course is not to show embarrassment but to have a flip comment ready that will demonstrate that you're cool. It is worth the effort to rehearse your handling of this situation, and to prepare a response that sounds spontaneous and will relieve the tension.

Men generally respect humor and don't feel that we have much of it. A quick wit is always appreciated, and if you handle these situations cleverly your presence will soon be accepted.

You may even raise the general quality of the humor.

Overcautious Boss

Bosses who find themselves supervising a management woman for the first time are often inclined to be cautious and overprotective. Supervisors win points by developing good people and lose points if they don't, so they probably want you to succeed. But they may have some typically male doubts about your ability to do so. They also know that they are responsible for the product of their department, including the goofs, so they may be concerned that your performance may not make them look good.

This type of boss protects himself in one of two ways, and sometimes both. Either he gives you the most simplistic assignments, to make sure you won't fail, or he checks everything you do in minute detail to make certain that it is accurate. In either case, you have little opportunity to prove how effective you can be, and you are denied that part of learning that comes from making mistakes.

Your solution in this case is to be direct. If you feel that your boss is being overprotective for your own good, tell him that you appreciate his concern and his desire to have you succeed in your work. Then tell him you strongly feel that your career development depends on your ability to demonstrate that you can stand on your own two feet, and that you would like to have the opportunity to do this.

If you feel that he doesn't have confidence in your talents, you might suggest that he give you a special project that will demonstrate your ability to do it on your own, but one that will not cause great repercussions if you fail. In other words, be straightforward about your desire for him to have confidence in you and about doing whatever you must to prove your effectiveness.

If you do this he can't fail to be impressed by your desire to do good and important work, and you may discover that he actually wasn't aware of the extent to which he was limiting your freedom of action.

Getting Hassled by Other Women

A woman on her way up in business is often in a double bind. She has problems with men in the organization who may believe her to be inferior, and she may also be hassled by other women. Remember, we women are not really taught to compete with other men but we surely are taught to compete with other women—for a husband, if nothing else. This is revealed by the way all of us size each other up when we meet, in terms of who's more attractive or who has the nicer clothes. Our competitive instincts with each other carry over into the business world.

One positive aspect of the women's movement is the extent to which it has begun to solidify relationships among women so that they can support each other in new ways. Despite this, you may still expect severe competition from other women in the office when you begin to move ahead. It is a problem you must confront directly and immediately, or your failure to do so will be interpreted as weakness and the competition will become even more intense.

Maryanne is a good example of a woman with this problem. She was hired as the first woman management trainee her company had ever had. In fact, it had never before had a woman employee who was not in secretarial or clerical work.

Instead of providing Maryanne with an office they put her at a desk in an area occupied by secretaries, eliminating any visible indication that her position was superior to the others. Maryanne had a college degree, but so did most of the secretaries. They were resentful when they were told that Maryanne was "special" and that they would have to type her letters and answer her telephone and take her messages. It was inevitable that Maryanne would be sabotaged, and she was. Her projects were the last to be done. She frequently failed to get her telephone messages, and when she did they were often incorrect.

Maryanne didn't know what to do. She feared that if she went to her boss and explained the situation he would conclude that she was weak. Eventually, she simply rode it out, experiencing a very bad time. Only when she was finally promoted to management and given an office, was her ordeal over.

She could have spared herself a lot of agony if she had done something about the situation the day she reported for work. Her employer had no previous experience with a woman in management and simply didn't realize the situation he had placed her in. The problem could have been avoided if she had asked him to introduce her properly to the other women as a management trainee, rather than having the secretaries feel that there was another woman around whom they had to cater to, without really understanding why.

Many women in clerical and secretarial capacities are jealous of others who have moved higher probably because they regret their own inability to do the same thing, and they resent her progress as a sort of silent accuser. They react by subconsciously doing what they can to contribute to her failure, which will make them feel less guilty about their own.

Idiot Assignments for Management Trainees

Women in management training assignments, particularly those who are the company's first woman trainee, often are given assignments so limited that they offer little opportunity for the development of skills. This is rarely because the manager of the program is intent on depriving them of the opportunity for growth, but because of unconscious assumptions that are part of the female stereotype. The male boss may, for example, feel that women are not career-oriented, and that it makes more sense to give the best developmental assignments to men.

A woman in this situation may be reluctant to protest for fear she will be viewed as a complaining female. It is also difficult to protest because what she considers an inadequate assignment may be viewed differently by her boss. If so, he will be extremely defensive if the situation is not handled correctly.

Nevertheless, it must be handled because unless a trainee is given real growth projects she will soon fall behind the others in the training class. She will be doing repetitive work that she already knows, rather than learning new skills that will help her grow. Despite the risks, it is not wise to accept a situation of this kind because, if you do, you will have a limited opportunity to move ahead. It is wiser to protest and lose your job than to stagnate in a situation like this. At least, if you lose your job, you are free to move on to a more rewarding situation.

Token Job—No Authority

Token jobs are much less common today than they were about five years ago, when the government first began taking action against companies who had no women in responsible positions. Some companies, however, are still hiring women off the streets into jobs that didn't exist before, in order to meet government requirements that they have women in all levels of management.

If you are in this position you are not really an employee but a statistic on the company's Equal Employment Opportunity report. You have a job but no real work, no real authority, and no real opportunity to develop your skills and improve your position in the company.

Unless you make the first move, the company is not likely to. A company like this has not yet decided that women can make a contribution in management, and it has simply decided to pay the price that is required to develop some minimally respectable statistics that will meet government requirements. If you want to improve your situation, you will have to take actions that will compel your employer to change his mind.

One very capable friend of mine who found herself in this situation immediately went to her boss and told him that she didn't feel that she had enough responsibility and that she wanted more. He agreed that he would give her more projects that were a real challenge, but they never materialized.

Her apparent choice was to remain parked on a dead-end street, or quit and look for a better opportunity with another company. Instead, because she saw opportunities in the company, she chose still another alternative. She took matters into her own hands and began a job enrichment program of her own.

Whenever she saw something that needed to be done she did it. She developed her own projects, set up her own schedules, and held her own meetings. As a result, her co-workers began to recognize that she had real talent and to depend on her for input. Before long her boss became aware of her contribution, and now she has another problem. She is so overworked that she hardly has time to breathe. But she loves it.

Discounting What You Say

You are in a meeting with five men with whom you are trying to solve a company problem. You offer a suggestion and nobody picks up on it, or even appears to hear you. Five minutes later one of the men makes the identical suggestion and there is a chorus of agreement. "Hey, Sam, that's a great idea." That's discounting.

The tendency of male groups to turn women off without listening to them probably comes from the stereotype that we women talk a lot without saying anything. But whatever the reason, it's terribly frustrating for those of us who have a contribution to make. The ultimate solution to being discounted, of course, is credibility. Once you have established yourself as having important contributions to make, people will begin to listen to you.

Until then, you can employ a few special techniques. First, many women tend to speak in soft, almost monotone voices. When others in the room are preoccupied with their own thoughts, a delivery like this is easy to ignore. Force them to hear you by speaking in a clear, clipped voice.

Second, make your comments direct and brief. We women are stereotyped as having to justify everything we say and, in the process, are seen to drag everything out. If you do this others will turn you off before your point has been made. Therefore, whenever you have an important suggestion to make, deliver it hard and fast. If explanation is necessary, someone will ask for it, or you can volunteer it later after your point has been made.

Third, learn the style that gets attention in each group in which you participate. Identify the male in the group who appears to be most effective in selling his ideas and observe how he does it. Then go home and practice that technique. Groups differ, and you must try to learn the style of presentation and interaction that is most effective with each one.

Small group dynamics are a fascinating and important aspect of business. If you want to get ahead your ability to understand what makes groups tick is very important, because as you move up the ladder the number of decisions made in meetings will increase in almost geometrical proportions. The ability to influence group decisions is a crucial one.

Your Boss Treats You Like an Object

It is characteristic of many supervisors and managers, who are burdened with heavy responsibilities, to overlook the human aspects of business. They are so preoccupied with their work that they forget the need for recognition felt by their subordinates. Nothing is more frustrating than to be doing effective work for someone who doesn't even seem to know that you exist. I have talked to many women who are convinced that their bosses think of them as machines—simply an extension of their typewriters or shorthand pads. They never say thank you, never talk to their employees except to give orders or ask questions, and never provide them with a sense of satisfaction in what they do.

In some cases this apparent indifference to people is simply the result of overwork under pressure, and the boss isn't even aware of his behavior or the reactions to it. In other cases bosses are uncomfortable with their secretaries and really are self-conscious about trying to relate to them as people. It is easier for them to act as though they weren't people and to concentrate on the tasks at hand.

Whatever the reasons may be for your boss's lack of human relations skill, it is up to you to change it. An approach that has worked well for many women is to do something so totally bizarre and foreign to your nature that it forces him to notice you. Once you break through to him, you will be able to develop a warmer working relationship.

The difficult part is making the initial breakthrough. One of my acquaintances brought her boss a funny caricature-type sculpture with a clever inscription that was appropriate to him. It made him aware of her as a person for the first time. Another actually sent a card to her boss that read, "Hey, remember me?"

A more adroit and acceptable procedure might be to go to your boss and tell him that you want to be as supportive as possible, but that in order to do it you need some feedback on how well you are doing. Tell him that if you were able to feel that he appreciated your work, your satisfaction might help you to do an even better job. When he thinks about it he'll recognize that this is really true. It's human nature to do more and do better when you know what you are doing is appreciated.

Eight hours a day, five days a week, is a big chunk of your life to spend around another person who doesn't know you're there. Work is much more satisfying if there is a positive relationship among you, your boss, and all of your co-workers. The others may not do anything to develop it, so it's up to you.

No Appreciation for What You Do
As long as the necessary work gets done, many bosses have no

idea of the range of activity that you handle. You will have a better chance of improving your position if you take steps to make sure that he knows everything you do. It's difficult for him to appreciate and reward the level of effort you are putting forth if he doesn't know the extent or nature of that effort.

Your position in a business organization is not unlike that of a wife whose husband thinks she spends her days lazing in bed or watching soap operas while he's off at work. It isn't until she gets sick or goes on a trip and he has to spend a day alone with the children that he has a true perspective on her activities. He didn't understand what his wife did with her day until he had to do it himself.

Obviously, you can't call in sick and ask your boss to do a list of things you had planned to do that day, but you can do the next best thing. Make a list of all of your tasks and the amount of time that you spend on each of them each day. Then go to your boss with the list and tell him that you want to be sure that you are spending your time wisely, and in the ways he wants you to. Ask him to review the list of activities and the time you are spending on each of them and tell you whether your priorities are right or wrong. This will force him not only to look at the list but to study it. You'll have scored on two points. He will have a better appreciation of what you actually do for him, and he will be impressed with your concern about whether you are using your time in his best interest or not.

11

Advice for the Recent College Graduate

Selecting your first full-time job when you graduate from college will be one of the major decisions of your life. Once you carve out that first foothold on your corporate Mt. Everest, you have probably made an irrevocable commitment to the mountain you will try to scale.

Have you ever asked an older man, locked into a business career that he has pursued all of his life, how he made the choice? Almost invariably the reply will suggest that it was "unplanned," "a matter of chance," "virtually accidental." Almost invariably, also, if you press him about whether he is happy with the choice he made, he will tell you that if he had his life to live over, he would do something else.

Although all of us have the option, at any point in life, to launch a totally new career, there are many reasons why most of us never do. The most important of these is the fact that once we have made our first career choice, we become terribly preoccupied with doing it well. By the time we get the urge to try a different field, we are so locked in by seniority, by the experience we have acquired that would be useless in another career field, and by our stake in pension plan and other employee benefits,

161

that either we lack the courage to make the break or it no longer makes sense to do so.

How Long Will You Work?

Even though a lifetime career in business may not be your present objective, you should think of your initial career choice as a lifetime decision and give it the thoughtful attention it deserves. The probability is that your choice will determine where in the country you will live, possibly for the rest of your life. It will determine how well you can afford to live—whether your wardrobe is from J. C. Penney or Saks Fifth Avenue. It will determine the kind of people you meet and spend your time with, and your position in society. It will determine how well you enjoy the third of your life that you will spend at work, and the kind of opportunities you will have to gain status, responsibility, and power. Even if you ultimately leave your first job and go to something else your experiences in it will subtly influence every aspect of your life in the future.

The evidence is that, in the past, most women who have graduated from college have not put much time into planning for their first job. After four or more years of school, they are eager to be doing something—maybe anything—else. They also may need immediate income, or they want to relieve their parents of the financial burden they have carried for so long. And in many cases, of course, they have the traditional expectation that they will get married, have children, and choose not to work.

Although most women do, indeed, have this choice, the statistical evidence is that even if you marry you will spend a substantial portion of your life working at some kind of job. In 1975, forty-four percent of the married women in the United States were in the labor force. Even with a break in employment, the average woman worker has a work-life expectancy of twenty-five years. If a woman remains single, her work-life expectancy is forty-five years—two years more than that of men! Given these statistical probabilities, it is fairly obvious that, whatever your current intentions may be, you should prepare for the possibility that you will spend a considerable portion of your life at work.

Career-Switching is Costly

Some women leap at their first job offer, rationalizing that decision by assuring themselves that if they don't like their first job, they can always switch to another. As suggested earlier, that is not always a viable alternative because when you switch career fields all of the experience you built up in your first job will lose most of its value. And, of course, the longer you wait to make the switch, the more you have to lose.

A career switch later in life also has a financial impact. If you have worked in one field for five or ten years, you will probably be earning more because of your experience. When you start over in a new field, you will be treated as a beginner and compensated accordingly. And instead of enjoying the advantage of experience over those just entering the work force, you will be competing with them as an equal in your new career field.

Reach Your Decision Systematically

In previous chapters, I have outlined a number of techniques that will help you make a sound career choice. I will not repeat them here, except to urge that you review those chapters and apply what you have learned. I've also talked about how to prepare for interviews and how to compose an effective resume. These skills, too, should not be neglected. What I want to reemphasize here, even though I've touched on it before, is the importance of setting priorities for your career and of making certain that the job you select meets both your work and your life needs.

Remember that the most important factor in deciding what job you want is knowing what is important to you in a job. Although your college education may have defined the broad career area that you will pursue, there are innumerable variations in the ways your specific education and skills can be applied. If you have a degree in accounting, for example, it may be used in many different areas of a company's operations, in many different circumstances. Some of these areas may provide real opportunities; others may be dead-end streets. Some may offer a real challenge; others may be repetitive and dull. Some may take you into areas where the action is; others may leave you stranded in the backwash of the company's operations.

Don't fail to use the techniques you have learned to define what your personal needs and priorities are and to identify the kind of activity that will give you work satisfaction. Consider whether you want a job that your present level of skills has prepared you to perform, or one which offers extensive opportunities for further training which may include some additional formal education. Know whether you want an eight-to-five job, or whether you are willing to make a larger commitment of time to achieve your objectives.

Advice from Others

You may already have asked for and received a great deal of advice from parents, friends, professors, advisors, and others. In fact, you have probably received a lot of advice you didn't ask for. Some of it may be genuinely helpful, but remember that when you are making a decision that will affect the rest of your life, your own needs are paramount, not theirs. Those who advise you are looking at what you should do from their point of view. That's all they *can* do. You are looking at it from another, highly personal perspective, because you are going to have to live with your decision from day to day. I am not suggesting that you shouldn't listen to advice, but once it has been given, process it carefully. Often, people give advice to others based on what they wish *they* had done. You cannot fault them for that, but it is your life you are concerned about. You may not want the choice they would have made if they had approached their first career decisions as carefully as you are going to approach yours.

How Long Should You Hold Out?

When they are offered a position, women graduating from college are often perplexed about how long they should hold out for a better one. They are fearful that if they delay their decision they may lose the opportunity and end up with nothing.

It is a gamble, of course, but all of life is a gamble If you delay accepting that first offer—or even if you refuse it—you may lose that one job, but if you accept it without careful consideration of the opportunities it offers, you may also lose not just a job but a lifetime of accomplishment.

How long you hold out will have to be a very personal decision, governed by a number of factors. One of them, obviously, is your financial need. Another may be the condition of the job market. If other graduates in your field are having difficulty finding positions, it may not be wise for you to sacrifice any opportunity that is offered. Still another may be the pressure being put on you by others—parents, creditors, for example—to go to work. The best advice I can give is to take all the time your individual circumstances permit to explore the full range of opportunities.

Questions to Ask During an Interview

Most young people, when they are invited to their first job interview, view it as an inquisition whose only purpose is to determine whether they are desirable candidates for a job with the company. It is that, of course, but that's not all. It is also your opportunity, as the candidate, to find out what the prospective employer has to offer you.

Don't fail, as suggested earlier in the book, to prepare thoroughly for your interview and have questions ready that will elicit information you want about the company and the job. Intelligent questioning on your part will also reveal to a male interviewer a degree of career interest that may rid him of any stereotyped view he may have of the level of dedication women have regarding work.

One of the most important things you will want to learn about any company you consider is its record in the employment and promotion of women. Very few companies at this point have significant numbers of women in management and executive roles, but you can get a feel for the corporate attitude toward women executives by observing the rate of increase of women in management over the past several years, and by finding out whether there is a structured program within the company to accelerate that rate.

It is possible, of course, if you are the type that likes to break new ground and feel you have the capacity to do it, that a company with a poor record might be ideal for you. Obviously, if you are offered a job, it is making an effort to change its posture, and if your performance with the company is effective and adroit, you may have a real chance to stand out and become a star. If you are less assertive, you will probably be more comfortable, and achieve greater progress, in a company that has a good record for promoting women into increasingly responsible management capacities.

A second crucial question you should ask is what kind of skills and talents you could expect to develop in the position for which you are being interviewed that would qualify you for promotion into more responsible jobs. Progress in business is largely based on the accumulation of skills, and it is important that you add to your skills at each step of the ladder.

You should also ask the interviewer to identify for you the kind of career path that might follow the entry level job you are discussing. What kind of progress has been made in the past by men and women who began their careers in this specific capacity, and where are they today? If high level responsibility is your ultimate objective, you don't want to begin your career in a dead-end job.

Many major companies now do career-pathing. Your interviewer should be able to give you a general outline of the promotional steps you will go through as you move toward the top of a specific job function. For objectives beyond that, career paths are somewhat more difficult to define at this early stage, since the skills you will need are acquired by branching out into other specialities or areas of company operations. In many companies, this broader experience is accumulated on the job, and the process is pretty much ad hoc. In others, it is achieved, in part, through management training programs.

That should be your next area of inquiry. What training programs does the company provide? Will you be placed in one immediately, or go directly to your job? If your career is to begin with a training program, how long will it last? Have there been other women in this training program and, if so, where are they today? If you are bored with school and eager to take on a real job, you may not do well if the initial training program is overly long. On the other hand, if you enjoy formal education, an extended training program may be just what you want and need to further prepare you to be more effective on the job.

Training programs fall into a variety of catégories; before you accept a job you should determine which types will be available to you. There are on-the-job training programs that are not unlike the apprenticeship programs for those entering craft jobs. Here you would have definite work assignments but someone would be responsible for supervising your work, teaching you how to do it better and grooming you to be fully and independently effective on the job. Then there is the "look-see" type of training program in which you have no specific job assignment, and are not responsible for any specific projects, but instead act as an observer who learns as she watches those in various departments do their work.

In management development training programs, you are rotated through various departments of the company. This may be planned to give you an overview of how your specialized function is performed in a number of departments, or to help you see how the many functions of the company departments fit together. These programs are particularly valuable if your formal training is highly specialized and you are not really sure which area of the company you would like to select as your major field of activity. The rotation provides an opportunity for you to make a choice, which will probably be given to you when you have completed the program.

Some training programs require classroom study and training sessions that complement the work that you are doing on the job. If you have had your fill of college work, you may want to know whether you will be involved in further textbook learning.

You should also determine what kind of assignment you will get when you have completed your training program. Will you immediately become a supervisor or a member of the management team? If not, how long can you expect to work before you achieve that status? Will you be assigned to a job at the location where you took your training, or will you and the other trainees be scattered throughout other company locations across the country? If personal considerations make it impossible for you to relocate, you don't want to become involved in a situation in which your upward mobility is tied to a willingness to work in any city to which you are assigned.

It will be clear from this description that different types of training programs will suit the needs of different candidates. You will have to determine which is most desirable for you. One option is to take a broad management training program in a large company, with a view toward moving someday to a smaller company that does not have its own training program, but where the breadth of your talents and experience will receive greater recognition.

If you don't know which type of training program is most suitable for you, it is wise to talk to a number of companies and compare the programs that they offer. You can also talk to friends who have gone through corporate training programs and get their views. The important thing is to do everything you can to reach the right decision.

Line vs. Staff Activity

One of your most important decisions will be to determine whether you want to go into a line or staff function. Line management is concerned with decisions related to the operations of the company—manufacturing, marketing, etc. Staff functions are supportive of line operations—market research, personnel, advertising, and the like.

For the most part, those in staff positions are specialists whose education and training were directed toward that function. Rarely are they rotated to line management positions, and the outer boundary of their career is the top position in their specialized function. Line managers, on the other hand, are often rotated in and out of various staff functions to give them broader experience in preparation for eventual executive responsibility.

It is obvious from this description that if your ultimate objective is to become chief executive officer, you should direct your career into the line rather than the staff. On the other hand, if performing a specialized staff function is what you enjoy, you should recognize its limitations. If your interest is personnel, for example, your career ceiling would most likely be "vice president—personnel."

Only in the last five years or so have women really begun to consider—and to be accepted in—line management roles. Today, however, a very real opportunity exists in this area, and if your quest for responsibility and upward mobility knows no limits, you will probably want to opt for a line rather than a staff position.

Deciding Among Job Offers

After you have interviewed with a number of companies and have a feel for the kind of positions that are available, it is time to reevaluate your career objectives. You can do this most effectively by employing once again the decision analysis technique. List the companies you have interviewed and also your work needs and priorities as you now see them. You will probably find that some have changed and that new ones have been added to the list. For example, you may have discovered that one of your concerns is management style. You have observed that some of the companies you have interviewed appear to have a very conservative management while others are quite freewheeling. You will want to determine which style appeals to you most, and which of the firms you talked to fits that style. You may also have discovered that different advantages are offered by the choice between a small company and a large one.

At any rate, crank all of the variables into the equation, and evaluate each company you have interviewed in relation to them. When you have finished you should know which of your job offers has the most appeal to you.

A Final Word of Caution

It is always possible, depending on the condition of the job market at the time of your graduation, that choosing among job offers may not be your problem. There may be none from which to choose. Yet you will be faced with a need to be productive in some way and to generate some income.

Be extremely careful in determining what interim employment you will select as a holding action until your real career choice is open to you. Many women, because they often know typing and shorthand, elect to use their skills in a secretarial job. Many of them conclude that this will give them "a foot in the door" from which they can advance to the first professional or management type of job that becomes available.

My advice, if you are tempted by this kind of choice, is to avoid it like the plague. The reason—female stereotyping being as prevalent as it is—is that once you have become identified with a clerical type job you will be positioned in your employer's mind as a clerical employee. This identification will also carry over on your employment record if you try to switch to another firm in the future.

Women have enough barriers to face in moving upward in a company without carrying with them the label of clerk or secretary. Although it is true that the government is pressuring companies to advance women from the clerical capacity to professional and supervisory roles in other areas, the same old barriers still exist in the minds of the men who make the decisions.

If you are compelled to take a noncareer-oriented job in order to eat and keep a roof over your head while you await a real career opportunity, I suggest that you explore the prospects in plant supervision or the craft jobs. Work in either of these capacities will not tie you to the female stereotype; in fact, it will help you escape it and enhance your prospects for a worthwhile job in your own career field.

12

Tips for Older Women Returning to Work

Erma Bombeck, the columnist whose ability to make light of difficult and annoying problems has brightened the day for so many women, addressed a column last year to women getting along in years who are dissatisfied with their position in life and wanting to change it. She wrote about a woman who "sat in her kitchen window year after year and watched everyone else do it and then said to herself, 'It's my turn'." She was writing about herself at the age of 37.

Ms. Bombeck noted that Margaret Mitchell won her first Pulitzer Prize for *Gone With the Wind* at the age of thirty-seven. Margaret Chase Smith was elected to the United States Senate at the age of forty-nine. Ruth Gordon got her first Oscar for *Rosemary's Baby* at the age of seventy-two. Grandma Moses began painting at seventy-six. Shirley Temple Black was named ambassador to Ghana at the age of forty-seven. Golda Meir had just passed seventy-one when she was elected prime minister of Israel. And Anne Morrow Lindbergh, after spending a lifetime in the shadow of her famous husband, was forty-nine when she began questioning the meaning of women's existence and published her book *Gift from the Sea*.

171

If you are an older woman who is planning to return to work because you need to or want to, and if you have doubts about your capacity to do so successfully, you might begin a confidence-building effort by keeping these examples in mind. Maybe, when a revised edition of this book is published a few years from now, your name can be added to that list. For the moment, however, let's just concern ourselves with what your opportunities are and how you can take advantage of them.

The Age Barrier

As men and women grow older it becomes more difficult for them to find positions in business and industry. The laws prohibiting employment discrimination against otherwise qualified persons for reasons of age have been difficult to enforce because of the nebulous nature of the word "qualified." Although the government is attempting to define more accurately what it means to be qualified, by requiring that qualifications be objective rather than subjective, there are still many loopholes.

For older people with valuable business experience and judgment, or with skills that are in demand, age is usually not an important barrier. However, the less significant your experience, or the fewer and less valuable your skills, the more difficult your problem. The absence of skills is less a barrier for younger people, because many companies will hire unskilled young people with the expectation of training them to become effective workers over time. This is an investment they may be unwilling to make in older people because there are fewer years of work in which the expenditure can be recouped.

It is not difficult to appreciate the company's point of view. Training costs money, and the most efficient use of the investment is to make it in those with long-range employment potential. Because of this the older person seeking employment should try to bring to it the highest possible level of existing skills, and to make certain that those skills are recognized by the prospective employer. The skills you have or are able to acquire are most valuable, of course, if they are also the ones that are in shortest supply.

This older workers category is one in which higher-level

executive men who are out of work have a more difficult problem than unemployed older women. Most executives hold their positions not because of the specialized skills that they have developed and maintained, but because of their abilities in decision-making and general policy areas. These skills may be salable, but they probably will be prized only in very special situations in the industry in which they were acquired, and only in a handful of top level jobs. There's only one president of General Motors.

This does not mean that an older executive male could not function effectively and be productive at a lower level. But many companies find it embarrassing to offer him that kind of position, or else they fear that he will not function well and happily in a position for which he is obviously overqualified and which he may find demeaning because of his previous business eminence.

How to Decide Which Way to Go

The older woman returning to work, or wanting to work for the first time, must determine first of all what her work needs are, what career choices she has that will satisfy them, what assets she has that will enable her to find that kind of employment, and what additional preparation may be required to achieve success. The self-analysis survey described in Chapter 2 may be used to determine your work needs, the work skills analysis to determine the skills you have and those you must acquire, and the decision analysis to determine which career path you should choose. Having done this you can then develop your personal action plan.

The type of job you look for should depend totally upon the priorities you set for your personal needs. These may include free time, money, a friendly social environment, business location, job challenge, security, responsibility or lack of it, choices in training for new skills, and other factors that concern you.

Let's say that your personal situation is such that your work needs include making a good salary in a location close to your home where you will be in pleasant and comfortable working conditions. In addition, you want to make friends at work, are not interested in taking on a lot of responsibility, and want to limit your working hours to the standard eight hours a day. You aren't really looking for management responsibility, now or in the future, and you would prefer a desk job to one where you are on your feet most of the time.

Based on this statement of needs and priorities, you might find that a clerical position fits your situation the best. You might be contented working in an office at tasks of a more or less routine clerical nature in a group of pleasant and friendly women with objectives and backgrounds similar to yours. However, if money has a high priority you will want to find the clerical job at the highest level of skill that you can handle, because you want higher pay. If you can qualify as a typist you will make more than a file clerk. If you can take shorthand you can make more than a typist. If you have high level shorthand skills you may be able to qualify as an executive secretary—a position for which older women are usually preferred.

Should You Invest Time and Money to Increase Your Skills?

If you are working primarily to alleviate boredom by having something to do, you may not want to invest any of your non-working hours in skill training—or to spend the money that it will cost. On the other hand, if income is critically important to you, or you want a more challenging position in your area of activity, you may very well conclude that the potential rewards are worth the investment. In this case you will get the training you need to upgrade your present skills and acquire new ones so that you can move upward in the clerical category.

Here's another example. Let's assume that it is imperative that you earn a high salary. You are an active person who doesn't like sitting at a desk, and you like to direct people although you have never done so in business.

Let's assume that you are not greatly concerned about your work environment and have no physical limitations that restrict the distances you can walk or the time you spend on your feet. You enjoy responsibility and want to gain a sense of accomplishment from your job. Salary, finally, is a major consideration.

As a general rule, the highest salaries are earned by those who have a high level of education and skill or who are willing to work at essential jobs that most others don't want. You need to earn as much as you can, but you have no special skills and your education ended when you got your high school diploma.

Obviously, in this situation, your greatest opportunity will lie in an area of employment that does not appeal to most people. Here you have an additional advantage because you are a woman. Companies are being pressed to hire women into non-traditional jobs and will get credit for hiring you in that kind of job, rather than in a traditional clerical or secretarial capacity.

Your entry point might be an unskilled job in a manufacturing operation. If your performance is above average you could then work your way into a training program and look forward to being promoted to supervisor in a relatively short time. Now you would be earning a good salary in an active job that would give you the satisfaction of directing the work of others. You don't mind the plant environment, you are learning new skills that will help you to continue to improve your position and your compensation, and you are also rewarded with the knowledge that you are doing something productive with your life.

Let's look at another example. To this woman, money is not important. She and her husband live comfortably, their children are grown, and she is simply looking for an activity more rewarding than bridge parties and teas. She wants to broaden her social contacts, but she is not interested in a lot of responsibility because her major interest is her home life. She does, however, want to feel that what she is doing is worthwhile.

This woman has a wide variety of opportunities. She can look for a job she will truly enjoy doing, regardless of compensation, because money is not a concern. Thus, if she enjoys books and reading, she might work in a bookstore; if she likes working with animals, a pet store would be an excellent outlet for her work needs; if she is socially concerned, she could accept a job at minimal pay with a charitable organization.

The differences in these three cases emphasize the importance of clearly and carefully defining your work needs.

How About Additional Training?
Many women who want to work in business, whatever their age,

are handicapped because they don't have usable business skills. Until recent years most women bound for college have not considered how their major subject could be applied in a business career. As a consequence, even the older women with college degrees usually have humanities or social science majors that have little or no value in the business world. While companies are, in some instances, willing to hire younger women right out of college and put them through training programs to learn useful skills, they are reluctant to do so with older women.

The type of training that would provide you with skills immediately usable in the business world would be greatly dependent upon your business interests. If, for example, you're interested in a secretarial position, you obviously will learn typing and shorthand. If you enjoy figures and detail work, you could go to a business college and take some accounting courses. This would allow you to do bookkeeping. If computers interest you, there are short courses that will prepare you for work in this area. If you have a definite skill to present to a company, in a type of work that is in demand, your chances of finding a position that you will enjoy are far greater.

If real estate interests you there are opportunities available for salesmen and brokers. You can enter this career by taking a course that will prepare you to take the license examination so that you can obtain a job with a real estate firm. Instruction is also available in many mechanical fields if you want to try for a non-traditional job.

If your interest is a position in a supervisory or management capacity, the problem becomes more difficult. Generally, there are no acceptable courses that train you to be a supervisor, except the in-house training provided by some companies. The best route to take would be to apply for a plant supervisory job and work your way up. Maturity is an asset in this kind of work.

Should You Go Back to College?

If you have the time, resources, and inclination you might consider getting a degree in business administration. There are many options today for the woman who wants to complete her college degree. Although a degree may not be important at the entry level, it may help you to reach a higher job level later in your work life.

Some colleges and universities offer programs that schedule classes on the weekend. There are correspondence programs which offer a four year degree. In addition, there are relatively new options such as life experience credits. This program, which is offered by a number of schools, allows you to earn credit for life experiences. There are requirements that you must fulfill, but the typical program does enable the older woman to get credit for self-education acquired outside the classroom. Many schools allow you to take examinations in specific disciplines such as math, humanities, or psychology, and if you score well they will give you credit to fulfill the course requirements toward your degree.

My advice to women I counsel is to get a college degree if at all possible because it widens your opportunities for advancement, provides you with a feeling of growth, exposes you to new and interesting friends, enlarges your perspective, and most important of all, increases your self-confidence.

The Importance of a Resume

You will want to follow all of the guidelines laid down in Chapter 4 on resume preparation. However, if you have been away from business for a number of years or have never worked at all, it is important to stress any kind of volunteer activities you have been involved in. Emphasize the skills you acquired in these capacities, using business terms (such as coordinated, advised, or organized) to make it clear that your volunteer efforts were businesslike activities. In effect, many of the skills are the same. For example, coordinating a meeting of volunteers requires the same skills as those used in coordinating a business meeting. But unless you point it out the corporate interviewers may not see it that way.

If you must work for financial reasons say so, and, if you are widowed or divorced, include that information also because it indicates that you have a financial need to continue working. Don't let the prospective employer think you want to work for pin money, because that is another stereotype that turns men off about working women. If they believe you are working for pin money it will be difficult to convince them that you are serious about a business career. Be specific about your intention to stay in the business world until retirement, and if you intend to go back to school or get additional training be sure to say so in your resume. That will indicate further interest in growth and job continuity—which is contrary to the stereotype men have of older women.

How to Find a Job

My earlier advice on finding a job applies to older women as well as young ones, but if you are widowed you should also consider contacting the friends in business that you and your husband have known through the years. They will be sympathetic to your problem and may be of great help in finding employment opportunities in their own companies and helping you get them.

At the outset, you might consider going to work for one of the temporary employment services, assuming that you have usable skills such as typing and shorthand. This type of service will send you out on temporary assignments with various employers, providing you with income while you sharpen up your skills. While on temporary assignment to a corporation, you may be able to find a permanent job.

Advantages of an Older Woman

It is important that you begin your search for employment with confidence. It may help if you recognize that while there are disadvantages to being an older applicant there are also some advantages. One of these is the fact that older persons convey a greater impression of reliability. Managers who began their careers in the past generation sometimes tend to think of today's young people as being less reliable than they themselves were when they were young. They will see in an older person someone brought up with their own values, someone who will feel under a greater obligation to perform well and diligently.

If you are successful in convincing a prospective employer that you are serious about working for the rest of your life, he or she may be attracted to you because of the feeling that, at your age, you are less apt to leave because of spouse relocation than would be the case with a younger woman. The possibility that the company might lose your services because of pregnancy also is less likely.

13

Strategy for the Career Woman

The career woman is one for whom I feel a special affinity, for she probably is a woman very much like me. She intends, for the present at least, to make business a lifetime pursuit. She has probably already identified her initial major goal and the career path that leads to it. She considers herself to be part of management and is determined to move up the ladder.

If you are in this category most of what you have already read applies to you, but some of my suggestions deserve emphasis. And I want to add a few more that may be of particular importance to you.

Specialization or the Mainstream?

Most of the women who have attained some initial status in business have done so by being highly qualified in an area of specialization. If your greatest joy in working is tied closely to the specialty you have chosen, your lifetime goal may be one of achieving eminence in that field. Perhaps you want to make a major scientific contribution and achieve prestige without power.

On the other hand, if you have a real need to attain a position of responsibility and authority, it is important for you to be

181

aware of the limitations of your specialized field. If you remain in it, your corporate stature will almost certainly be limited to the top company position within the specialty that you have chosen. That is why less than five percent of today's middle managers are women.

The typical career in general management moves you upward from an initial rather narrow experience, in a technical or specialist's role, to broader and more conceptual responsibilities for making decisions and solving problems that concern the company as a whole. Fundamental changes in activity and responsibility occur as you move through various levels on the corporate organization chart. The specialist applies her knowledge to the solution of specific problems. Supervisory duties are closely related to task completion. The middle manager coordinates the activities of her function with other company functions. Senior managers are less involved with day-to-day activities than with long-term objectives and policy formation. And at the very top, the chief executive is concerned with policy determination, major decisions related to financial planning, capital expenditure, and other matters that involve the long-term welfare of the corporation. A considerable portion of the chief executive's time is spent on functions that are largely ceremonial.

When you understand this structure it becomes apparent that the career path leading to senior management requires this initial transition from the specialist to the broader and less precise position of middle manager. For women, this is a difficult path to follow.

Men in business are supported, as we have observed, by a male culture of shared beliefs and expectations, and they are taught, tested, and promoted through largely informal systems that are still overwhelmingly controlled by men. Although most men also begin as specialists of one kind or another, they are soon able to expand their horizons and begin to build experience in other functions that prepare them for broader management roles.

Because women, unless we are unusually assertive, are generally excluded from the all-important informal developmental systems, we often find ourselves pushed into the back room of the corporate structure. Unless we are content to remain specialists we must find ways to work our way into the informal systems or develop management skills on our own.

Find a Mentor

I have already discussed the mentors or godfathers who provide support for most successful male executives. Your chances of breaking into the male-dominated informal systems will be infinitely greater if you can find one, too. The importance of a mentor to a businesswoman was illustrated by a recent Harvard University study of twenty-five high level women. Every one had attached herself very early in her career to a particular male boss who served as her mentor. History, of course, is replete with famous women who also had male mentors—among them Margaret Mead, Simone de Beauvoir, and Elizabeth Barrett.

A mentor can become the influential advocate who enables you to crack the informal structure of the company. Meanwhile, he counsels and guides, provides you with access to the important information already available to male peers, and supports your career ambitions through his relationships with those in the upper reaches of the company organization.

Associate with High Producers

This is a strategy most ambitious young men learn early in their careers. Observe the "comers" in your company. Whom do you see them with in the corridors, at coffee, or at lunch? Almost invariably it will be other "comers" like themselves, or higher level executives who have influence and are admired throughout the company for their effectiveness on the job.

These men are engaged in a process that Phil Drotning calls "status by osmosis." They are very conscious of whom they are seen with because they know that if they are consistently observed in the company of other men who are effective performers, those with power will conclude that they must be good performers, too. They have learned that to be seen in association with marginal performers or troublemakers is not smart business strategy.

This behavior may seem distasteful to you, but remember, it is an integral part of what you are trying to learn—the male business game. If you need rationalization before you can behave this way yourself, simply acknowledge that all of us can learn more through association with effective people than we can having lunch with a table full of losers.

Who's Your Competition?

A corporate organization is shaped like a pyramid of people. As you ascend it you will find fewer positions at each succeeding level, with one King Tut at the top. Consequently, your chances for further promotions decline in inverse proportion to the successes you have already achieved. The competition becomes increasingly fierce as you move ahead.

When you chart your career path, take a hard look at the others in the company with whom you will be competing at each stage of your progress, and also at the incumbents who are already there. Is the top slot filled by a person close to your own age, so that there is little hope that it will open up before you, yourself, are almost ready to retire? Is the path blocked along the way by a relatively senior employee who perhaps has reached his level of incompetence and will be stuck there for the remainder of his career? If so, perhaps you should take a second look and pick another career path, or the same path in another firm.

Typically, women in business have not paid attention to this kind of detail; we become aware of our predicament when it is already too late.

Avoid Using "Feminine Wiles" to Get Ahead

A group of 200 male executives, asked to list their objections to women in business, ranked the exploitation of sex as number one. The stereotype does perceive us as using our "feminine wiles" to get ahead, and it is a perception that it is essential to change.

Barbara Boyle Sullivan, partner in the personnel counseling firm Boyle-Kirkman Associates, said it well: "The bedroom is not the way to the boardroom. If your boss or your associate asks you to dinner and there's no business reason, forget it. Keep your personal life out of the company."

Increase Your Influence

I define "influence" as motivating others in the direction of your desires. This is largely a function of status and visibility, both of which can be developed if you put your mind to it. Here are a few tips:

Try to develop business relationships with executives in the company who are recognized as having authority and power. Your association with them will add to your own stature.

A strategy many males employ is making influential people in the company aware of what they are doing by distributing carbon copies of their more important letters and reports to executives who have a legitimate interest in the subject. Over time they come to be seen as making a significant contribution.

Another element in the male game plan is discovering the special interests—business or otherwise—of senior executives. Then look for appropriate articles in obscure publications and send them along with a buck slip stating, "Thought you might be interested in this." The executives appreciate receiving the information and, even if they perceive the real motive for sending it, will probably admire the initiative.

Enlarge your job by picking up bits and pieces of work that are being neglected by others. You will find many unmotivated people in business who are happy to have others do their work for them. If you accumulate enough additional duties you'll have a bigger job, and management will begin to see you as a "go getter" who picks up the balls that others drop.

Be aware that as a woman interested in a career, your constant task is to break out of the traditional business female stereotype. You must not resemble women employees who have chosen the traditional clerical/secretarial roles. You already have a problem because so many men perceive women only in this capacity, and it is not wise to reinforce that stereotype by associating with clerical women at the office.

Identify the formal and informal groups and committees that are considered influential and attempt to gain admission to them. The members of such groups are usually those already identified by management as high potential people, and you will have an opportunity to learn a lot about how to "get things done." The dynamics of a group of high potentials offers invaluable insights to success in your company.

Company Training Programs

Many companies offer in-house training programs designed to broaden the knowledge and skills of narrowly specialized employees who are in management or have management potential. If your company has such a program and you believe that you are ready for it, ask that you be included. Because the employment of women in professional capacities is a relatively new experience for many companies, it is quite possible that no woman has ever been included in one of these programs and it may not have occurred to the men in management that one should be. Make them aware by asking that you be included. Even if you don't succeed the first time you ask you'll soften them up and make them see that you really have a long-range career interest with the company. The next time you ask, they may be mentally prepared to grant your request.

Self-Development

Another way to emphasize to your superiors that you are career-minded and growth-oriented is to initiate your own self-development program. One good technique is to suggest additional special projects that will broaden your knowledge of your own department and enable you to learn other aspects of the company's business. Better still, identify a project that would be of value to your boss and the company and just go ahead and do it. If it is a worthwhile project and the work proves to be of value, you will project your image as a productive and highly motivated employee.

Because the development of additional skills and broader knowledge of the company's operations are essential assets in your efforts to climb the career ladder, the time may come when you are becoming stagnant in your present assignment and need to develop in other areas. Emphasize your desire to increase your knowledge and skills so that you will be more valuable to the company.

This is an action worth taking even if it is a lateral position with no increase in salary, provided the new position will significantly increase your promotional potential.

Intentional Learning

Some of the skills that foster upward progress are not readily learned through structured methods of training. An example is the skill of "meeting influence"—the ability to persuade a group of your co-workers to your point of view in decision-making situations. An excellent method of learning a skill such as this is intentional learning, which most women overlook completely.

Intentional learning is a process by which you determine precisely what you want to learn and then identify those around you who possess that skill or attribute. At that point it becomes a simple matter of observation. Study the others as they use the skill you wish to learn, analyzing how they use it, when they use it, and with whom they use it. You may even approach these people directly and ask them to help you learn the skill they know. You may be surprised to find that they are proud of their talents and skills and flattered that they have been asked to share their knowledge with you.

Develop an Effective Meeting Style

The meetings in which you are asked to participate can offer one of your most productive opportunities to get ahead. Be prepared for every meeting you attend, and don't leave one without making a significant contribution. These are highly visible situations in which to gain recognition, often in the presence of those with the power to help you gain promotions.

My friend Colette, who is now a rising star in the Chicago business world, once told me that early in her career she was often silent and unprepared in meetings because she was unaware of their importance. Then one day, while she was talking to a young man already marked as a "high potential" employee, he excused himself to go to his office and "figure out how to take over a meeting."

She asked what he meant by that remark and he explained that he had been invited to attend an important meeting and needed time to prepare the contribution that he would make. He said he also wanted to analyze the others who would be present so that he would be able to counter their objections effectively.

Colette was astonished, but she got the message and now she's on her way up, too.

In addition to intentional learning, you can develop meeting influence by taking a course in small group dynamics. A course such as this will teach you the fundamentals of much of the behavior that is displayed at meetings. An understanding of the interaction process will help you to become more effective. You can also learn this skill by joining organizations outside of business, and volunteering to head committees or subcommittees so that you can practice various chairmanship styles.

Your ability to be effective in meetings becomes more important as you move up the corporate ladder because the broader your responsibilities become the more meetings you will have to attend. At the middle management level your ability to influence your peers from other functional areas becomes of prime importance. How you communicate with them and win their support can make the difference between effectiveness and mediocrity at the middle management level.

Should You Go Back to School?

The best preparation you can have for a general management career, in my opinion, is a Master's Degree in Business Administration. The MBA is highly valued in business because it provides a general theoretical background into which you can place the specific work content of your job. It also enables you to understand how your job and functional area fit into the overall structure of the company. The need for this breadth of understanding increases as you move upward in the company and your responsibilities become more generalized.

If you are an active person with many interests other than work, the commitment of time to the pursuit of further education may not seem appealing to you, but you would be wise to explore it further. The educational process has been greatly modified in recent years to accommodate to older men and women who already work. Most of us think of higher education in terms of classrooms, lectures, examinations, and grades, but while our attention was elsewhere the process has taken on new dimensions, as explained in Chapter 12. If your hangup is the feeling that "I'm too old to go back to school," visit a night school classroom. When you look at the students you'll regain your long lost youth.

Change the System or Play the Game?

After thirteen chapters of Sharie Crain you know where I'm coming from, but I also know something about you. You really want to succeed in business or you would have closed the book on me long ago.

It would be rewarding to believe that we have the capacity to change the business system—the rules of the game—so that we could begin to play it our way. Realistically, that option is not open to us yet because the power in business is still held by the men who made the rules, and if we're going to win the game we'll have to play it their way—at least for a while.

I hope I've helped you learn the rules so that you are ready to play. You'll find that it's an exciting game.

14

The Future for Women in Business

In the years ahead, more of us will join the work force, responding to new freedoms, economic pressures, and the needs of business itself, and more of us also will continue to educate ourselves in business-oriented disciplines. It is inevitable that we will almost imperceptibly assume roles at all levels of management—not simply because of governmental pressures but because of fundamental changes in our social and cultural environment.

What will this mean for us, and—perhaps more important—what will it mean for business? Will we continue to accommodate ourselves to a business system invented by males in earlier generations, or will business change to encompass our talents and sensitivities, assets that have, until now, been considered liabilities?

My guess is that business will change—in attitude if not in structure—because society will demand it, and that women will be a vital force in helping it to change.

In the aftermath of the 1976 presidential election, a perceptive editorial writer in the Chicago *Daily News* commented on a phenomenon of the campaign that was generally overlooked. It is one that may be the harbinger of change in cultural attitudes. He wrote:

"It seemed that almost every time we turned on the tube, especially in the later hours, some man was crying. And while this may have been a campaign to make strong men cry, that just hasn't happened before, at least not in public.

"But there was Jimmy Carter wiping away the tears, Jerry Ford doing likewise, for a different reason, Big Jim Thompson [governor-elect of Illinois] choking up to the camera, and others caught in the glare of the TV eye unashamedly letting their emotions show. Even Bob Dole, between sessions of living up to his reputation as a hatchet man, was shown breaking into sobs as he expressed his gratitude for the loyalty of his hometown friends. And there were others.

"We're not quite sure what to make of all this, but it does seem to mark a trend away from the long-held notion that men don't cry. Most men have been taught from childhood that crying is unmanly; emotions must be bottled up, not expressed; only women cry. If this barrier is now breaking down, it could be one of the most significant outgrowths of the 1976 election, worthy of study by psychologists and sociologists as well as politicians.

"Was it only four years ago that Senate Edmund Muskie lost in New Hampshire because he shed tears in the snow and the cameras caught him at it? Maybe he was just a man ahead of his time. This year he would have been in good company, and right in style."

There is a moral there, not in the fact that powerful men can cry without being demeaned by it, but in the fact that human sensitivity—so long excluded from the male businessplace—is becoming an acceptable behavior pattern for men. If Mr. Gallup and Mr. Roper and Mr. Harris are right about public attitudes toward business, I can only say, "It's about time."

I am convinced that in the years ahead business will change and that women will find a more significant place in it because American corporations need the superior sensitivity and intuition of women to respond to a new level of public expectations. Historically, little has been demanded of business and industry beyond the production of reliable and useful goods and services at fair prices and in quantities that met an almost insatiable public appetite for convenience and luxury. Few expected businessmen to solve social problems ("The business of business is business") except, perhaps, those created by and within their own operations.

During the past decade or so there has been a significant evolution of public expectations of the business role, although too many corporate typoons still have trouble accepting it. The very success that business has achieved in satisfying the material wants of the nation has led the American people to believe and expect that these same talents, energies, and resources can now be turned to the solution of the social ills that plague us. Meanwhile, we also see a new range of expectations for recognition and self-fulfillment on the part of those who work within business itself. The failure of business to respond adequately to those expectations—the tendency to continue "business as usual"—is at the heart of the public opinion polls that demonstrate a steady and potentially disastrous decline in public respect for and confidence in American business and the economic system within which it functions.

The times call for a new type of businessperson. I predict, in the decade ahead, that increasing numbers of top business executives will be women. As a woman, I delight in the knowledge that many of the traits that have been culturally induced in us (and programmed out of the male psyche) are the very traits that may be essential to the survival of business in the future.

I find it fascinating that much of the group dynamics and sensitivity training now being given to corporate executives is designed to expand their consciousness to include what are essentially female traits—traits that they instinctively reject when they perceive them in businesswomen. Most men who enter business already possess the traits needed for low and middle management; analytical skills, competitive instincts, the capacity to plan, organize, coordinate, and control. The conventional business wisdom has always been that these are the traits and capacities required to reach the highest levels of managerial authority, that these are the essential keys to successful performance at those levels.

New research suggests that this is far from the case. Studies of managerial behavior by such well-known researchers as Richard Neustadt, Sune Carlson, Leonard Sayles, Henry Mintzberg, and many others suggest that successful executives rely less on the logical, linear functions of the brain, less on coldly analytical processes than on more holistic, relational, intuitive skills that are less typical of men than of women.

Mintzberg, for example, in two superb articles in the *Harvard Business Review,** notes the propensity of successful managers and executives to rely on "soft" rather than "hard" data in the decision-making process. He observes the extent to which managerial input is "soft and speculative—impressions and feelings about other people, hearsay, gossip, and so on." Managers favor verbal communications, which enable them to "read" facial expressions, and tend to synthesize rather than analyze the information that they process.

Managers, in discussing the process of making strategic decisions, rarely report using explicit analysis. They use words like "hunch," "intuition," and "judgment." A student of public policy-making, Yehezkel Dror, has written:

"Experienced policy makers, who usually explain their own decisions largely in terms of subconscious processes such as 'intuition' and 'judgment,' unanimously agree, and even emphasize, that extra-rational processes play a positive and essential role in policy-making."

In short, the higher the level of authority one reaches in business or government, the less the reliance is placed on rational analysis and strategic planning, and the more that is placed on "soft data" and intuitive processes in the course of making decisions. This does not mean that the hard data is ignored, but simply that it is only one component of a thought process that relies heavily on less firm data as well.

What this suggests to me is that while we will continue to struggle to achieve at the lower levels of management, *we may be better equipped than our male competitors to succeed at the upper levels.*

---

*Henry Mintzberg, "The Manager's Job: Folklore and Fact," *Harvard Business Review*, July–August, 1975, and "Planning on the Left Side and Managing on The Right," *Harvard Business Review*, July–August, 1976.

Women's greater intuitive skills, viewed negatively at the entry levels, will become a priceless asset in positions of corporate authority and power.

Nor is the future potential of women limited to white-collar jobs. Companies that have responded to federal EEO demands that women be placed in nontraditional roles are making some surprising discoveries that inevitably will affect employers' attitudes about "appropriate" work for women.

For example, the merchandising giant Sears, Roebuck and Company constructed a new catalog order distribution center in a Midwestern city. At the time the new facility was being staffed, Sears was contesting a charge by the federal Equal Opportunity Commission that it had discriminated against minorities and women. In response to this impending threat, the company decided to establish hiring requirements at the new plant that would accurately reflect the availability of minorities and women in the local labor force.

Initially, the recruiters found it difficult to interest women applicants in traditionally blue-collar jobs. However, when these candidates for clerical work were made aware of the higher pay levels in some types of blue-collar work, and the nature of the work itself was demonstrated to them, they began to respond. As a result, when the loading docks and warehouses began operations a third of the forklift truck operators were women.

That, in itself, was unprecedented, but soon the plant manager made an even more remarkable discovery. Losses due to the damage of merchandise in loading and unloading were significantly lower than those in similar facilities elsewhere, where the forklifts were operated exclusively by men. Why? One possible reason for the change, said management, is simply that women may be more cautious in the operation of vehicles.

In this case, putting women into a nontraditional job initially appeared to be a burden to the corporation but ultimately proved to be a bonanza. There are bound to be other, similar revelations as women are granted more opportunities in nontraditional areas—opportunities that allow us to demonstrate what we *can* do rather than what society has taught everyone to *think* we can do.

While we're waiting for this to happen, the first step is to make it at the lower levels by utilizing the techniques you have learned in this book. The timing is right and the opportunities are there for women who are willing to make the necessary psychic and time commitments, to prepare themselves educationally, and to keep up to date.

I don't want to imply that I foresee any early or sudden changes in the basic business system. Many observers predict significant operational changes as more of us enter the field of work—part-time jobs, flexible hours, team activities, and the like. I don't agree. The game won't change much for some time to come. But there will be enormous improvement in the opportunity for women to play it and win. There will be heightened appreciation of women in managerial jobs. Men will learn how to deal comfortably with those of us who have moved beyond supportive roles. Our superior intuitive and "people" skills will be increasingly valued at the top levels of management.

Most important, all of us will begin to play the game better because we understand it at last, and because we have learned the rules.